East Sussex Coastal Railways

Volume 1: The Ashford to Brighton

Paul O'Callaghan

First published in 2011 by S B Publications
Tel: 01323 893498
Email: *sbpublications@tiscali.co.uk*
Website: *www.sbpublications.co.uk*

© Copyright Paul O'Callaghan 2011

ISBN 978-1-85770-365-8

Layout by Vital Signs Publishing - email: *info@vitalsignspublishing.co.uk*

Acknowledgements

First and foremost I must thank my mother, Christine Weedon, for supporting me (due to my ill-health) on some of my walks. I would also like to thank Peter A Harding for providing me with the railway photographers. Of the railway photographers and suppliers of old railway photos, I would like to thank: Rod Blencowe (of the Lens of Sutton association), Sue Bowman (of Seaton Tramway), Bob Cookson, Richard Casserley, Alan Davis, Hugh Davis (of Photos from the Fifties), Alex Forbes, Mick Funnell, Roger & David Haggar, Hastings library, Lawson Little (of the Narrow Gauge Railway society), Roger Quantril, John Scrace, John Spencer (of THWART) and the Transport Treasury. In addition, I would also like to thank Jo Kirkham, and Lindsay Woods of S B Publications.

[Front cover: Loco 1060 at Norman's Bay, 1939 (see page 51). Photo: H C Casserley. Back cover: See captions on pages 6, 9 and 75. Title page: Unit 1001 at Rye, with the 11.24 Ashford to Hastings train, 10th June 1995. Photo: John Scrace]

CONTENTS

Beyond the End of the Line – An Introduction

From when I was a small child, I would (sometimes with my Mum) be driven down from south east London to Hastings by my Grandad Syd, with my Nan, on the grounds that my Nan fancied some fresh fish. To me Hastings was like the end of the world, as at the far end of the town was Rock-a-Nore Road, which came to a dead end where the land ran out. This end-of-the-world feeling about Hastings was emphasised after I became a railway enthusiast (1986/7), and noticed that the Charing Cross and Victoria to Hastings trains terminated at Hastings. To go eastwards, beyond Hastings, I imagined was to go 'beyond the End'. I didn't know the coastline west of Hastings, let alone east, so going west from there also gave me a similar feeling.

In 1988, my Mum, on our last trip to Hastings with my grandparents, went further up the East Cliff to see what was beyond (my grandparents would usually stop after going up the East Cliff lift). She returned, saying it was, "beautiful" over the hill top. It was in May 1989 when I finally went beyond the End: Arriving by train, my Mum and I planned on walking up the East Cliff and then going all the way along the coast at least to Winchelsea Station, if not Rye, where we would catch the train home. However, this was one of the rare occasions I misjudged the distance to walk and didn't realise there were three valleys to go through before Fairlight.

It was a hot dry day and, after passing down and up through Ecclesbourne Glen, we walked barefoot so as to get a grip on the dry earth. At Fairlight Glen I spotted a cove, and we began down the path to it to bathe. On nearing it, I let out an exclamation, "Muuuummmm!". I had spotted it was a nudist beach. We retreated back up to the path to Fairlight, where we had cold drinks at a café near the Church (still there today). We continued our journey on through Fairlight to Winchelsea Beach, now realising we were not going to reach Rye, and so planned on heading for Winchelsea station. By the time we reached Winchelsea Beach it was dark and late, so Mum began looking for a Bed and Breakfast to stay at. One woman took pity on us, even though her bedrooms were full, putting us up in a spare room overlooking the beach, giving us cheese on toast and telling her guests a brother and sister had turned up late with nowhere to stay (not the first or last time my Mum was mistaken for being my sister!). It was great, going off to sleep listening to the waves.

The next morning, we headed into Winchelsea, with the morning heat mist lifting and the Sunday Church bells being rung - one of the most perfect mornings of my life. After looking around Winchelsea we got to the station, discovering what a good idea it was that we had gone to the B&B, as the station was like a simple 'halt'. We caught the train, with no guard asking for tickets. We spent an enjoyable lunchtime and afternoon discovering Rye, before catching a train to Bexhill; my first time beyond Hastings in a westward direction. The beach was crawling with baby crabs.

In 1991 I returned to Rye for a day out to trace the old Rye and Camber tramway using Peter A Harding's book. A couple of months later I returned to Rye (Playden) for a holiday, which included my first East Sussex railway trip beyond Bexhill, so as to visit Seaford and discover Cuckmere Haven for the first time.

A few more days out followed, but I was struck by a terrible infection in 1994 and was medically neglected, so trips to the sea were reduced to twice a year if I was lucky. In 2005 I moved to Eastbourne.

Originally I had meant to write a book just about the railways beyond Hastings' eastern end. Now 'Beyond the End of the Line' applies to both lines beyond the Charing Cross-Hastings line. For practical reasons I have started the description of the railway route from the east going west

(from Ashford and Rye). Thus for the first time, the history of the East Sussex coastal railway is told in this book, which focuses on the main Ashford to Brighton line, and a planned Volume Two, which will explore the many connecting branch lines and nearby narrow gauge railways. Details of construction and openings are included here which will not found in any other railway book. Included is the Marshlink Rail Festival in 2007 and the campaign to save Three Oaks, Doleham and Winchelsea stations, together with the less well-known fact that, during the 1960s, campaigns were waged to save the Rye and Lewes–Brighton sections of line from closure. A description of the development of each station on the Ashford to Brighton line (including the lost St Leonards West Marina station), with old and new photographs, will also be found here.

Enjoy.

Paul O'Callaghan

Appledore Station, 25th April 1947, with the 10.54 New Romney branch train to Ashford.
Photo: H C Casserley

PART 1: Ashford to Brighton - A General History

Much has been written, and is still being written, about the main lines to Brighton and Dover. Because of this I don't intend to give a detailed history of the Brighton or Dover main lines - there are plenty of second-hand bookshops in Worthing, Brighton, Lewes, Seaford, Eastbourne, Bexhill, Hastings and Rye, where local railway books can be found on those. Instead, this book concentrates on sharing a lot of information on the thus far neglected Ashford–Brighton line.

As far back as 1816 (one year after the Battle of Waterloo), the first proposal was made for an "iron railway" between Shoreham-by-Sea (the nearest port to Brighton) and Brighton itself, which had become a popular destination for the aristocracy as the Prince Regent had begun to visit the town. By the mid 1830s there were six proposals being considered by Parliament to link London to Brighton. Brighton Vestry (Town Council) supported such a link, later favouring John Rennie's proposed route to London. Parliament, following its engineers' report on the proposed routes, also ruled in favour of Rennie. On 15th July 1837, the London & Brighton Railway Company obtained Royal Assent. This also gave the L&BR legal powers to construct a branch line to Shoreham-by-Sea and another to Newhaven, but the L&BR only bothered to construct the Shoreham branch, which opened first, partly so that locomotives from the north east could be shipped in.

The Shoreham Branch opened on 11th May 1840 (with public services beginning on 12th May). Hence it was on *this* date that the first Brighton Station opened. The London to Brighton Railway main line did not open until 21st September 1841. Trains used the L&BR tracks as far as Redhill, and then shared the tracks with the South Eastern Railway (the main line for which began here for Dover), the London & Croydon Railway from Norwood Junction, and finally the London & Greenwich Railway from Corbetts Lane junction (just over a mile east of London Bridge).

The South Eastern Railway opened its line through to Ashford on the 1st December 1842. The locomotive hauling the first train was called Harold and was described by a local press reporter as a "puffing monster". The line on to Dover was completed for opening on 7th February 1844. The East Sussex Coast line would, when completed, be the only one to join these two old main lines together, with one regular through service between them - but such a service would not be scheduled until November 2005.

Meanwhile, since 1835, the South Eastern Railway (which constructed the Redhill to Dover railway line) had been considering a branch to Tunbridge Wells, and other branches from Headcorn to Rye and Smarden to Hastings (the route for the latter was even surveyed). In 1846, there was another proposed railway to start at Smarden and to be built through Tenterden and Rye to Hastings.

The best-publicised proposed-but-never-built line was promoted by a Mr C Ferwen. His line would have passed through Tenterden, from Headcorn to Hastings, with a separate branch to Icklesham and Rye, costing £307,000 (though this proposed cost was reduced to £250,000 following criticism). It was to be built by the Tenterden, Rye & Hastings Branch Railway and this company would lease itself to the SER. However, in 1844, the SER decided NOT to back Mr Ferwen's line, as it failed to pass through any large towns. Henceforth, the SER only wanted a railway to Hastings to go via Tunbridge Wells. A deputation visited the SER on 12th April 1844, calling for it to construct its line to Hastings via Tunbridge Wells. The following month a report was prepared for a railway to Tunbridge Wells and the SER began buying up land southwards to Robertsbridge.

This sudden flurry of activity by the SER was influenced by a Parliamentary Select Committee ruling in favour of a railway to Hastings from Brighton. This helped give the Brighton, Lewes & Hastings Railway company (BL&HR) the Act to construct its line (the present day Brighton to St Leonards line). The Act also stipulated that this new company must sell its line to the London & Brighton Railway. The legal powers to construct the Newhaven branch were also passed to the BL&HR, which opened its line from Brighton to Lewes on 6th June 1846, and then to a point between St Leonards and Bulverhythe (where the company built a station, St Leonards West Marina) on 27th June (a Sunday). This reduced passengers using the horse-drawn coach to Staplehurst Station for the SER London train. The contractor for the whole line was George Wythes (constructing the Brighton to Lewes line for £7,000) and the engineer was John Urpeth Rastrick. A Victorian, Robert Kent, gave an account of seeing the first train from Lewes arrive here (he described the station as a "temporary ramshackle kind of a structure on the Salts of Bulverhythe") when the line opened in 1846:

"Most of us had never before seen a train and some of us hardly knew, either from hearsay or pictures, what it was like, so I need hardly tell you that when it was seen approaching there was NO little excitement. The whole of the station being practically open, and there being no buildings, we of course could see it as

it wound its way in. It was not till four years afterwards that we at Hastings had a station, so that during all this time the fish intended for out of town transportation had to be taken to the station at the Salts".

The L&BR (the parent company of the BL&HR) showed an interest in having its offspring company extend on beyond St Leonards to Rye and Ashford. This was the SER's self-styled territory. The SER promptly panicked at this threat and began having a route surveyed for a railway from Ashford to Hastings. However, in October 1844, the SER had applied for a Bill (the application for an Act) to construct a railway from Headcorn to Rye, with an extension to Ashford, but dropped the idea of a Headcorn to Rye line. The Board of Trade (BoT) objected to a direct railway line from Tunbridge Wells to Hastings, so granted the BL&HR the legal powers to construct the line to Ashford via Rye.

The BoT had been influenced by the government and the Duke of Wellington no less. After the conflict with Napoleon just thirty years earlier, Parliament still felt Romney Marshes were difficult to defend (having constructed the Royal Military Canal and Martello Towers along the coast for the same reason). A railway passing across the Marshes to Ashford would enable troops to be conveyed by train quickly to fight any invasion in the Marshes area.

Loco 1775 at Ashford locomotive shed, c. 1938 (Paul O'Callaghan collection)

The SER was not about to give up the fight to own the line to Ashford. So, on the one hand, it offered to construct the Hastings to Ashford line for the government (in return for its granting the construction of the North Kent Line through Gravesend), while on the other it persuaded the BL&HR to relinquish its legal right to own the line to Ashford, following the SER settling disputes about Redhill with the L&BR. The BL&HR was pleased to hand over its legal rights, as the line passed through thinly populated areas and only the small town of Rye, so the company did not expect much use of the line. The government, however, had granted permission for the SER to construct its Tunbridge Wells to Hastings route, but on the condition that it did not open until after the Ashford to Hastings line had opened.

The Brighton Vestry had publicly supported the Brighton-based railway company controlling a coastal line from Portsmouth to Dover, which would result in trains travelling from those destinations via Brighton, and not some other railway company which did not serve Brighton, with the Vestry specifically mentioning the London & South Western Railway. Whilst the Brighton company would have the most direct line to Portsmouth (until the LSWR built its line from Guildford), the Vestry were to be disappointed about having a Brighton company have its own line to Dover, as now the route was to be given to the South Eastern Railway.

On 27th July 1846, the London & Brighton Railway and the London & Croydon Railway merged, creating the London, Brighton & South Coast Railway (LBSCR), though it could be interpreted as the L&BR gobbling up the L&CR. This company would last until 1922.

Now, with its self-styled territory of Kent protected, in 1847 the SER set about trying to avoid constructing the Ashford line to Hastings through the Ore area, so that they would not have to dig any expensive tunnels. The SER had

already obtained legal powers for a branch line from Lidham Hill (on the edge of the Brede Valley, near Doleham) to Whatlington, just north of Battle. The SER's proposed Tunbridge Wells to Hastings line was to pass Whatlington, so it hoped to cheaply continue the Ashford line along the Brede Valley (which it was following from Rye anyway) to Whatlington, and then use the Tunbridge Wells line to access Hastings. However, in November 1847 the SER told the LBSCR that it had dropped the plan to have a Lidham Hill to Whatlington line!

The proposed deviation to Whatlington would have cost £10,000 per mile. Contractors Wythes had been lined up to build it, having offered to do so for £55,524.00, but in 1848 the deviation was dropped due to Parliamentary opposition, so the SER was forced to finish the line along its original route (through Three Oaks and the Ore area), finally requiring the reluctant digging of two tunnels to reach Hastings, with the line rising steeply uphill to Ore before descending down to Hastings.

In January 1847 the SER decided that King & Spivey should construct the Ashford to Rye section, for £122,956.

Construction of the Line

The biggest construction project for the BL&HR line was the London Road (formerly Preston Road) viaduct, just east of Brighton. Built of ten million bricks (the first brick laid by the chairman's wife in May 1845), it is 400 yards long, with sixteen arches making a massive curve to a radius of ten chains [see page 75]. The viaduct piers are tapered, the northern arches wider than the southern ones in order to keep the sides of the arches parallel. The longest span arch is 50ft (across the London Road), whilst the highest point from the ground is 67ft. The viaduct took ten months to construct and was finished in March 1846. John Rastrick was the engineer overseeing its construction. A stone balustrade was built to improve its look. The military Martello Towers (Numbers 43 and 44), built to defend Britain from an invasion by Napoleon, were demolished in 1845 to make way for the Bexhill–St Leonards railway.

Under the agreement with the SER to take over the Ashford line, the BL&HR had agreed to dig what is now known as Bo-Peep Tunnel and construct St Leonards Warrior Square Station. The geology here is the sands of the Hastings beds and Wadhurst clays, which had to be dug through to create the 1,318 yard Bo-Peep Tunnel. The shafts for the tunnel were sunk in September 1847. During 1848, construction temporarily ceased due to the houses above losing water from their wells, creating springs in the tunnel. The digging proved difficult, resulting in a sub-standard size, lacking inverts, which meant that trains were only allowed to pass

each other in the tunnel from 1885 until 1906 - in effect only one of the two tracks was used.

Whilst Bo-Peep Tunnel was being dug, in July 1848 the Board of Ordnance approved Mr G R Stephens' plan for a bridge across the Royal Military Canal near Warehorne to carry the line from Ashford. By 10th August, the Admiralty had approved a railway swing bridge design (by Peter Barlow, the engineer) across the Rother at Rye, which was then constructed by Ransome & May.

By September 1848, the line from Ashford to Rye was ready for opening, and the hop-planters called for it to be opened. However, the BoT refused permission, wanting the rest of the line to be completed first so that it could all be opened in one go. In addition, the SER had opted to open the line as single track, but prepared the beds for double track, which it would acquire later. In September 1850, the SER decided to open stations at Ham Street, Appledore, Rye and Winchelsea.

Brickmaking sprang up in Hastings as part of the preparation for constructing the line to Ashford. A Miss Mackay placed the first brick in Hastings Tunnel on 24th July 1849, whilst the next day Captain Barlow's wife placed the first brick in St Leonards Tunnel. The bridge over Queens Road is constructed of iron fluted columns, erected in 1898 [see page 41]. Until then, a tunnel (probably like that beneath the Hastings line at Orpington) for Ore Lane had existed in the long embankment from the station to Hastings Tunnel, carrying the railway. There had been a lot of concern about the Ore Lane area being blocked up at the time of the line's construction, and this concern probably continued, forcing the railway to include the tunnel and bridge.

The Opening Degenerates Into Farce

The SER decided to have the ceremonial opening on 28th October 1850 - before the railway was finished! This was to

St Leonards Tunnel, seen from St Leonards Warrior Square Station, 1996. Photo: Paul O'Callaghan

enable the Lord Mayor of London, formerly of Hastings, to open the line before his term as Mayor ended. Because the SER deemed the Mayor's opening of the line the most important priority, before it was even safe to travel on, let alone complete, the following events occurred:

Firstly, due to torrential rain, workmen had to prevent the rails from sinking into the mud using hand-spikes, whilst the ceremonial train passed over them (could one imagine this happening for the Channel Tunnel link line?). Secondly, as it passed through the Romney Marsh stretch, the train appeared vulnerable to being blown over in the gales due to the instability of the line.

Despite this, along the route from Ashford to Rye, lots of people cheered the train. At Appledore, the Mayor from London was welcomed and made a warm reply. Green boughs hung at Rye station. Flags flew from the church and roofs of houses and ships. During the day, bells rang out. The Mayor arrived at Rye at lunchtime at a temporary platform near New Rope walk, accessing his horse and carriage (brought down for him from London the day before). He was welcomed by Jeremiah Smith, the Mayor of Rye. The two Mayors, with officials on horses behind their carriage, then made their way to Mayor Smith's home, where more people greeted them and the ceremonial lunch was had. The London Mayor later retired to the George Hotel, where he enjoyed a further sumptious dinner. However, after the ceremonial speeches at Rye, the train continued on as far as Guestling where it had to wait for an hour - not to let another train pass, but because the track was not finished!

Upon arrival at the middle of Ore Tunnel (lit by candles), a stage had been set up for the Lord Mayor to climb on to insert the last brick in the tunnel's lining. But afterwards, the train needed men and horses to get it going, finally reaching Hastings three hours late. The Lord Mayor finished by inserting the last bricks into both tunnels either side of Hastings.

It is not surprising that the LBSCR had applied for an injunction blocking the opening of the line on the grounds of safety (though whether this was their true reason, or to stop competition, is open to debate). The SER had hoped to open the line to the public on 1st January 1851, but the BoT inspector refused permission due to poor signalling facilities and a lack of ballast (a lot of which could have been Dungeness shingle, as that was the only local source for ballast). He again refused in late January. The Ashford to Hastings (Bo-Peep Junction) line finally opened on 13th February 1851, the bells of St Clement ringing for the opening all day.

It was because the first trains to London from Hastings would go via Rye, and not Tunbridge Wells, that the junction at Ashford was constructed facing in the London direction.

The Bo-Peep Battle

The junction west of St Leonards was named Bo-Peep after a nearby inn visited by shepherds from the marshes. However, the Bo-Peep of the nursery rhyme is no representation of the battles the SER and LBSCR fought at Bo-Peep, which developed into another farce.

In January 1851, before the Rye line opened, the SER had contacted the Railway Commissioners to establish if the LBSCR would have a legal right to put its staff at Hastings Station. The LBSCR, meanwhile, had legal rights to run its trains into Hastings Station as a result of the agreement with the SER to have the Ashford line. The reason the LBSCR wanted to exercise its legal right was that passengers riding trains to London would be more likely to use them than the SER's trains to London via Ashford, which was a longer route (the SER's route to Tunbridge Wells would not be finished until the next year). The SER no doubt recognised this. Thus the SER signalmen, upon the opening of the line to Ashford, promptly refused to allow LBSCR trains to go through to Hastings. The LBSCR, on protesting about this to the SER's Superintendent, who happened to be in the area, was informed by him that he had no legal confirmation that the LBSCR was the legal successor to the BL&HR, and told that the signalmen required a timetable of LBSCR trains, which the latter swiftly supplied. Everything appeared fine for the day after opening (Friday), but, that night, workmen ripped up the track, preventing access to Bo-Peep Tunnel, whilst a slow moving wagon train of soil blocked access to Hastings' sidings, leaving the LBSCR train of two locomotives and seventeen carriages (for use the next day) marooned. The LBSCR's representative at Hastings even had his gas supply stopped in his office.

The LBSCR countered by operating a horse-drawn bus service from its St Leonards West Marina station, to the SER's St Leonards Warrior Square. The SER then blocked the buses from entering the station yard and took legal action against the LBSCR staff for trespass and against the LBSCR for a lack of legal documentation. The LBSCR in turn took court action, winning an injunction against the SER in March. The SER claimed to have blocked the line due to the LBSCR allegedly spreading rumours that the soon-to-be opened line to Tunbridge Wells was not safe. In truth, this new line was a threat to the LBSCR's income from Hastings passengers.

The SER had also wanted to split the income from Hastings passengers using both the Lewes and Ashford routes to London evenly, as the LBSCR was carrying more passengers on its line than the SER was. An agreement to share receipts was agreed on 1st February 1852. The tension rumbled on between the two companies, as the SER accused the LBSCR of using St Leonards Warrior Square as a goods station (the LBSCR was not allowed to stop passenger trains there until 1870), instead of Hastings, so losing the SER revenue. During 1853, the LBSCR paid £642 in tolls for use of the SER line from Bo-Peep Junction to Hastings. The SER did propose a station at Bo-Peep Junction for £4,800, but gained no support from the LBSCR, as the latter had its legal rights to run into Hastings Station. So the SER constructed West St Leonards Station. The Ashford to Hastings line did not earn its own upkeep until 1895!

In 1871 catch points were installed at all goods sidings between Ashford and Hastings, and Ore Station was opened on 1st January 1888.

The 'Halt' Services

In 1899, the SER and its Kent rival, the London, Chatham & Dover Railway, put aside their differences and set up the South Eastern & Chatham Railway Managing Committee. To increase passengers on the line it was decided to begin a new type of service. This was a steam railcar service; basically a single carriage fixed to the rear of a steam locomotive (other companies had petrol locomotives), which ran a service between Rye and Hastings. It was for this service that 'halts' were opened along the line, a halt being only long enough to accommodate a single carriage, unstaffed and with only a shelter - basically a very cheap station. The use of the word 'halt' was phased out in England and Wales in the late 1960s. The railcar operated six times a day around 1910. In 1913, this had increased to ten services a day, two going beyond Rye to Appledore.

For this service, Three Oaks, Guestling and Snailham halts opened on 1st July 1907. Snailham is now closed, its up platform appearing to have been replaced by a concrete version. It was located at the end of a farm track. It was not named after the Giles cartoons (of the *Daily Express*) where the British Rail slogan, "quicker by rail", was accompanied by a picture of a snail... Snailham was, in fact, named after the local farm. It was closed on 2nd February 1959, having opened as Snailham Crossing Halt. In fact it was Eastbourne Station which received a cartoon of a train there being hauled by a snail!

Three Oaks opened as Three Oaks Bridge, but the 'Bridge' reference was soon dropped. As Guestling was closer to Three Oaks Halt than Guestling Halt, the former was renamed Three Oaks & Guestling. Guestling, meanwhile, was renamed Doleham after a nearby farm. Doleham (like Three Oaks and Snailham) cost just £295 to construct. There are still three road signs, which refer to it as "Doleham Halt" [see page 35].

The SER board had considered, but not acted upon, an

Three Oaks, with rail motor train, c. 1910 (Paul O'Callaghan collection)

idea for constructing a station for Guestling in October 1883. A second attempt for such a station was made in 1898 but was rejected.

Meanwhile, the London, Brighton & South Coast Railway had the same idea for developing increased passenger use of its Eastbourne to St Leonards West Marina service. It began a railmotor service earlier than the SECR, on 14th September 1905, opening halts for this service at Stone Cross, Pevensey Bay, Normans Bay, Cooden Beach, Collington Halt and Glyne Gap. Each of these halts were built as simple affairs: platforms made of wood and lit by oil lamps. The service

Normans Bay c.1934 (showing the now demolished crossing keeper's cottage)
Photo: H C Casserley

began on 16th September 1905, a wet day. Later on, halt platforms were extended and shelters added. Stone Cross Halt was closed in July 1935, while Glyne Gap Halt had shut down as early as 1915 (a local passenger group at Bexhill had hoped that this halt could be reopened, but concentrated instead on keeping the important London train service running to and from Bexhill).

These services were again basically a carriage fixed to an engine, with two of these four trains being petrol driven and the other two steam powered. All were third class and could carry 48 people. People wishing to get off at a halt, had to inform the guard, so he could stop the train for them. Smokers had a separate part of the single carriage train. The seats were poorly made, as it was third class only (three-ply birchwood with an oak frame), but there was some decoration. Panelling was cream coloured with vermilion and olive green borders. The pilasters were made of oak.

In 1909, Lord Brassey led a delegation calling for a through coastal service, which the SER promptly provided, with a train running from Margate to Brighton once a week. In 1923, the LBSCR, the SER and LCDR (with the London & South Western Railway) were forced by Parliament to merge into the Southern Railway, which rebuilt Hastings station [see page 41]. From 27th November 1949 until 5th June 1950, a bus service operated between Hastings and Warrior Square, and Crowhurst and Bexhill West, as Bo-Peep Tunnel had to be closed for repairs. Trains from Tunbridge Wells were diverted using the Crowhurst to Bexhill West branch line via Sidley, terminating at Bexhill West, whilst trains from Brighton terminated at Marina Station.

The Beeching Effect and Later Cuts

In 1963, the infamous Dr Richard Beeching report was published, proposing the closure of two-thirds of Britain's railways. Amongst these was not only the New Romney Branch, but also the Ashford to Hastings line. The local press reacted with the heading, *Beeching Cuts Out All Romney Marsh*. In 1969, the aptly-named Transport Minister, Richard Marsh, gave permission for closure of the line if a replacement bus service was established. A campaign was launched to save the line.

In 1967, British Rail's operating costs for the Rye line were:

A) Operating Trains - £84,000
B) Stations - £40,000
C) Tracks & Signalling - £187,000
D) Interest on capital value and administration - £58,000
Total: £369,000
Earnings: £59,000, plus a grant of £310,000

When this costing was publicly released in March 1971, the Ashford to Hastings Rail Users Association disputed it, pointing out that BR had ignored the profit from freight trains and receipts of passengers coming from beyond the line.

In 1970, it had been expected, unsurprisingly, that the line would close, but it received a two year reprieve, following financial savings made by replacing staffed level crossings with automated ones, and singling the track between Appledore and Ore in 1969, leaving only a passing loop for trains at Rye. But the ex-SER line wasn't the only line in danger of closure. During the early 1970s some expected the railways to Lewes, and even to Shoreham, to shut, so a major campaign was started in May 1972 to ensure more use to keep them open. This was the decade of Miss World competitions, so a 'Miss Coastway' competition was launched and a Coastway Dance was held where the winner would be announced. This is where the 'Coastway' title for the Shoreham and Eastbourne lines originates from. A £100 prize was offered for the best six reasons for keeping the lines open. The Ashford–Hastings line, meanwhile, soldiered on into the Network South East era (1986–1994), appearing in an article in *The Independent* in 1990. Trains calling hourly at Ham Street, Appledore, Rye, Three Oaks and Ore were met with a strange but unforgettable image of a silhouetted figure in a hat, in a marsh. (If anyone knows what this was supposed to represent, then please get in touch. It would be nice to have this figure back just for the logo.)

In 1994, British Rail ceased to exist due to privatisation, with the track, signals and stations becoming the property of Railtrack (now Network Rail). The operation by BR of Kent train services, known as Kent Coast, became the responsibility of the South Eastern Train Company, whilst the Sussex trains were provided by South Central (so readying these parts of BR for privatisation). However, in 1995, South Central took responsibility for the former Kent Coast Rye line service. Connex (now infamous for losing the franchise in 2000) was the first private train company to operate both the Kent and Sussex lines, which are now run by Southern (an old name, re-launched). In 2006 the Marshlink Community Rail Partnership (set up to improve the old SER Ashford to Hastings line) was extended to cover the Hastings to Eastbourne line via Bexhill.

Many of the slam-door DMU trains, which ran on the Ashford-Hastings and Uckfield railways and were replaced only recently, have found new homes on heritage railways such as the Spa Valley at Tunbridge Wells.

In November 2005, Appledore lost its hourly service, which shocked even the national railway magazines. However, after a short campaign by local people, the station regained its full service. However locals are not relaxing, as their parish magazine is putting out appeals to its readers to use the station to maintain its future (it would no doubt help if the station name carried the subtitle, "for Romney Marsh Villages").

A local campaign group, THWART (Three Oaks and Winchelsea Action for Rail Transport), was set up in the area along similar lines to the 1971 group, to save Three Oaks, Winchelsea and Doleham stations, as they feared the running-down of services was a pre-cursor to permanent closure, as had been the practice since the 1950s. They pointed out that two of the three trains a day were at 5.00am

and 10.00pm, making them no use. Southern stated that a survey in 2005 found a lack of use at the three stops. It also stated that because most of the line is single track it prevents an increase in train services (as the trains can only pass at Rye). Clearly, if custom was not too thinly spread between these three little-frequented stations, then the surviving one (or ones) would have greater use, once the new service was advertised to locals.

To increase trains, a passing loop could be created at Three Oaks using the partially-existent second platform, which would help increase services on the line without the need to double the line. Currently Three Oaks lacks a bus service, and the nine miles from Hastings to Doleham, and Winchelsea to Hastings, has no evening bus service. The Three Oaks & Winchelsea Rail Action Group (led by John Spencer of Winchelsea and Monika Betson of Three Oaks), having protested at the three stations as trains whizzed through on the Community Rail Festival of September 2007 [see page 33], successfully achieved having fourteen trains a day stop at Three Oaks and Winchelsea stations. One train in the first hour stops at Winchelsea, but not Three Oaks, then in the second hour the next train stops at Three Oaks, but not Winchelsea, thereby providing both stations with a train every two hours.

The Eastbourne Branch Line

For Eastbourne residents, there was a horse-drawn carriage omnibus operating from the yard of the New Inn in South Street, Eastbourne, to Polegate and back. This was run by Mr D Burford of The Anchor public house.

Until the 1840s Eastbourne had been a small town, consisting of what is now Old Town and Sea Houses, along with the hamlet of Southbourne. At the time of the opening of the Lewes–St Leonards railway, the primary landowner was William Cavendish, a member of the aristocracy, carrying the title Second Earl of Burlington. In 1834 he owned two-thirds of Eastbourne parish (as well as owning estates in Lancashire), as this was when he inherited the Compton estate. He gained the additional title of Duke of Devonshire in 1858 upon the death of a cousin.

Cavendish's support for a branch line from Polegate to Eastbourne was part of a plan to develop his land for housing development. The branch line was to have been constructed further to the west, closer to the South Downs, but due to the cheapness of the land it was instead laid further eastwards. The engineer was John U Rustrick and the contractor was George Wythes, who built the line for £27,811. There were originally two over-bridges (near Eastbourne) and nine under-bridges. The branch is four miles, 23 chains long, and begins with a falling gradient out of Polegate for three miles of its length before entering a rising gradient of 1 in 521, which increases to 1 in 267. The curve into Eastbourne was a tight 40 chain radius, until the station was moved. The level crossing across Lottbridge Drove (later renamed Willingdon Crossing) was installed from the outset.

The branch opened on 14th May 1849. The *Sussex Express* reported the opening day as follows:

"On arrival of the train at Eastbourne, a large concourse of people were waiting, and we were received with great

An ex-Eridge loco passing Eastbourne's coal yard, 1947. Photo: Sid C Nash
(Bob Cookson collection)

enthusiasm, added to which a brass band was playing, 'See The Conquering Hero Come' – a most appropriate welcome, as doubtless the steam engine has been one of the greatest of all-conquering heroes in the advancement of civilisation.

A large party sat down to an excellent cold collation provided by Mr. William Parsons, the host of the Gilbert Arms."

According to a young George F Chambers, recalling the event in his book of 1910, when he had become a barrister, he stated the luncheon was held in a large booth in the grounds of Orchard Farm (which by 1910 was where Orchard Road had been laid out), the home of Mr Smith, the steward for Lord Burlington.

The *Sussex Express* continued;

"The party were led by Mr. Freeman Thomas Ralin. Amongst the party were: Sir William Domville; Sir M. C. Smith; Captain Willard; Reverend W. W. Robinson; G. Ballie Esq; Colonel Witeman; Messrs R. B. Stone; W. Rasom; Robert Boys; J. T. Filder; John Filder; Alexander Hurst; Plummer Verrall (Lewes); James Barry; Charles Simmons; Daniel Burford; and others."

Sports and a "grand display of fireworks" concluded the evening. Mr Chambers reported that the fireworks were of "amateur make" by his uncles, Mr F Brodie and Dr D J Hall.

The first trains to Eastbourne included Third Class carriages, which lacked roofs and even seats, the better rolling stock reserved for the higher social classes! The opening of the branch line had a slow effect on helping Eastbourne develop as, in 1851, builders of the new housing and hotels had difficulty finding tenants for them. Cavendish had to put forward money on each of the new houses, but still the builders entered bankruptcy. By 1859, the total spent by Cavendish was £37,000, and he lost interest in developing the town. However, on inheriting the title of Duke of Devonshire later that year, he began once again to develop Eastbourne. He employed a new architect who designed Devonshire Place, and extended expansion into the Meads village area in 1872. It was also in 1859-60 that the branch line received a second track along its length.

The Branch Becomes a 'Y'

Until 1871, trains operating between Brighton and St Leonards which stopped at Eastbourne had to reverse back up the branch to Polegate in order to proceed along their journey. Thus a link line to give direct access from the branch to the mainline facing Pevensey was required. The authority for the Willingdon Loop, the link between what is now Hampden Park and Stone Cross village, was given on 1st August 1870, opened on 1st August 1871, and improved in 1872. It is one mile, eight chains long, the junction with the Eastbourne Branch being named Willingdon Junction (after the village to the west of the railway), and the junction with the main line as Stone Cross Junction.

Thus, from 1871, the Eastbourne Branch became shaped like a Y: Eastbourne at the bottom; Polegate at the top left corner; Stone Cross at the top right corner. Later, Hampden Park would be added in the centre. The Brighton–St Leonards railway continues to pass through Polegate, and then straight on through Stone Cross. On 6th January 1969, due to a lack of use, the up track of the mainline between Polegate and Stone Cross junction was removed, so all passenger trains from thereon all went into and out of Eastbourne on the branch, with only departmental trains using the down track between Polegate and Stone Cross, to avoid Eastbourne. This ceased in 1974, when the down track was disconnected at the Polegate end, rendering it as just an engineer's siding, until it was fully lifted in August 1984. Today just the track bed between Polegate and Stone Cross survives.

The Community Rail Festival

The Community Rail Festival was held at Rye on 29th September 2007, and at Hastings, Ham Street, and Ashford. Whilst Ashford Station had a display about Ashford's railway heritage, Hastings had amusements and Ham Street had a local author reading to children. It was at Rye where the main events were happening. Getting up before dawn to oversee it all was young Samantha Bryant, Marshlink Development Officer, who ran a Marshlink stall with her colleagues at Rye. Other stalls consisted of local produce and local heritage railways (Rother Valley, Spa Valley and Romney, Hythe & Dymchurch Railway). The RHDR had laid some track in the car park (the former goods yard) to run a locomotive, 'The Bug', with a carriage to give rides.

Visitors view the author's display at Rye Station (Paul O'Callaghan collection)

'The Bug' loco pulling a train on temporary tracks at Rye Community Rail Festival, 2007. Photo: Paul O'Callaghan

Inside William Tress' historic station building's booking hall were a collection of photographs and historical facts (supplied and written by myself) about the Ashford to Hastings line (plus a photo by a gentleman called Gary, and another person's display about Uckfield station). A special Marshlink ticket was issued on the weekend for £10.66, enabling the buyer to travel anywhere, getting on and off the train, between Brighton, Tonbridge, Maidstone, Canterbury and Dover. Leaflets also carried coupons for the weekend to visit local historic establishments and other tourist places where for two people, one could get in free. Importantly, as the trains zoomed through Three Oaks, Doleham and Winchelsea stations, at each station about a dozen people waved placards and shouted, registering their protest at only having three trains a day on the Marshlink line since the service was extended to Brighton in 2005. At Rye station a tent housed a petition stall to save the stations and increase the trains.

Currently, at Ore, Ashford-bound trains go onto the down track so as to continue their journey, because the up track only exists beyond Ore as a siding for electric trains from London Victoria, Charing Cross and Brighton, which terminate at Ore. The electric third rail runs out at Ore. By having the up track and electric rail extended to Three Oaks, trains from Charing Cross, Victoria and Brighton, which currently terminate at Ore, could instead go on to terminate at Three Oaks.

Loco 32636 at St Leonards West Marina, 29th March 1956. Photo: H C Casserley

PART 2: Ashford to Brighton - The Route and Station Histories

Ashford Station

Ashford is the biggest hub of train services in Kent, so unsurprisingly it has the biggest history of the stations on this line (there's even a railway book solely about Ashford). So to leave room for the story of other Marshlink stations, here is just a brief summary.

Ashford Station began as part of the SER main line from Redhill to Dover (only the third line in Kent), which opened in stages, starting with the section of line from Headcorn on 1st December 1842. The line was opened through to Folkestone on 23rd January 1843. As we saw in Part 1, the first train to Ashford departed London Bridge at 9.00am, hauled by a locomotive named Harold, described by a journalist as a "puffing monster", which was met by a band at Ashford. The station originally consisted of two platforms, with possibly four tracks between them. Its first footbridge wasn't installed until 1845, costing £150, and it had wooden station buildings. Its first rebuild (the decision for this being taken soon after the line to Canterbury opened on 16th February 1846), saw an enlargement during 1848-9, with the platforms being lengthened in 1851. In March 1853 the rebuild was found to have cost £267,433, so to

cope with both the Canterbury and Hastings lines' traffic, extra goods facilities were added in 1856, including a siding for the cattle market. Yet another rebuild took place by 1865, the wooden constructions being replaced by red brick buildings, which some locals may still remember. It also had two extra platforms added. It had been estimated in January 1863 that this work would cost £15,000. In 1869, tenants operating the station refreshment room were charged £250 per year. On 1st November 1891, the London, Chatham & Dover Railway had its line from Swanley to Ashford linked to the SER line, with all passenger trains ceasing to use the LCDR Ashford station from 1st January 1899 and using the SER station instead, as Ashford residents had wanted for many years. In 1907, the station was rebuilt once again, gaining extra platforms and sidings.

Ashford was rebuilt for the penultimate time, ready for electrification of the Dover line, in 1961-2, with the two bay platform tracks being extended westwards along the platforms to re-join the main line platform tracks on the west side of the station, so creating two island platforms with four tracks in-between, but with two loop tracks, the former bays, on the outside. This necessitated the

ABOVE: *Thumper 205012 Ashford to Hastings (right) and Ashford to Charing Cross (left), 25th August 1988. Photo: John Scrace   BELOW: Ashford Station, August 1991. Photo: Paul O'Callaghan*

demolition of the red brick station building, being replaced by the modern building on the north side. This station lasted until 1994-5, when Ashford was rebuilt once more, a new island platform being built on its north side where the 1961-2 station building was. This was so that the station could accommodate Channel Tunnel trains.

An engine shed was given the go-ahead for construction by Barlow in February 1845, ready for the Canterbury line opening. In January 1899, the SECR agreed to an £80,000 deal to centralise their wagon and carriage workshop at Ashford, buying up 60 acres of land. It opened in 1902. This was then complimented by having the locomotive construction works centralised at Ashford (planned in 1911). Staff transferred from elsewhere to Ashford to do this job in 1913.

A new engine shed was opened in 1931, covering ten tracks. Some of the works continued in use until 1988, after most of it shut in 1962. (To the west of Ashford a carriage and repair shop was opened in 1960-1.) It briefly became the Ashford Steam Centre (an early steam heritage centre) in 1969, but this closed due to a dispute. The clock tower at the locomotive works is now listed, and parts of the shed survived into 1994. During 2003-4, there was talk of reviving the steam centre.

Ham Street Station

On June 23rd 1848, the residents of Warehorne village petitioned the SER for a station and received Ham Street. Following a request in 1851 for full goods facilities, a goods shed was built in 1861 and the viaduct was rebuilt for £3,500. The station had, like the three other original stations, staggered platforms (not opposite each other), as it was believed that it was less likely for passengers to be hit by the train they were departing if they used a foot crossing behind the train.

Ashford train arriving at Ham Street, 18th June 1958. Photo: H C Casserley

Ham Street, looking south, June 2006. Photo: Paul O'Callaghan

The main station building was designed by William Tress in the Italianate style, which used to have a signal cabin (more like a garden shed) on the south end of its up (Ashford) platform. Oil lamps, though out of use, survived into 1974. It has a low pitched roof and a veranda platform with a slate roofed canopy (added years after the building was completed), which extends around the south side of the building and above the public entrance on the west side (although it doesn't go around the wider Station House part of the structure). It is a twin of Winchelsea Station building. Unusually, the front entrance to Station House is shielded by a storm porch, the door having two steps up to it.

The station was renamed Ham Street and Orlestone on 1st February 1897 (one of the station's signs with this name could still be seen in Adams newsagents/bookshop in Rye High Street, along with other old station name boards, in 2007).

A wagon turntable lay opposite the up platform, whilst a replacement signal box with sliding windows was at the north end of the down platform, where the foot crossing is. The bridge over the Royal Military Canal was replaced in 1902. South of Ham Street is Warehorne Crossing, which had a crossing keepers cottage, the crossing gates being replaced by automatic ones in 1981.

One and a half miles north of Ham Street is Rucking Crossing, which was provided with a crossing keeper's cottage (similar to that which survives at Appledore). A public goods siding was laid in June 1884. This was complemented by a siding for storing a super heavy gun train, which could fire shells across the Channel. A further siding for such a gun train was laid at Hollybush to the south and Golden Wood to the north. All were laid by the War Department.

A locomotive belonging to the contractor Wythes exploded at Ham Street on 30th April 1852, killing driver John Hadley as he stopped to check the boiler (part of it struck his head). A drawing of the remains of the locomotive can be found in the Wakeman Collection at Ashford Library.

Appledore Station

Appledore was also designed by William Tress. The goods shed, which still stands today, was built in 1896 for £830, beside the up platform, the platform canopy being added after it was constructed. Between the goods shed and Tress' station building, the Gentlemen's was constructed. The signal box used to be located just before the junction with the New Romney Branch, which opened to the public on 7th December 1881, but finally closed to passengers on 6th March 1967, though freight and nuclear waste trains still use the remaining part to Dungeness (an excellent history of the branch can be found in the 2007 booklet, *The New Romney Branch Line* by Peter A Harding, available in Rye

Loco 1306 at Appledore Station with the 11.32 train to New Romney, 25th April 1947. Photo: H C Casserley

shops). In preparation for the opening of the branch, new semaphore signals were installed in 1881, lasting until 1987. The signal box was replaced by one beside the level crossing opposite Tress' building on 27th June 1954 and was still in use in 1991, but it has since been demolished. On the opposite side of the road to the site of this box, the crossing keeper's cottage still survives. So many have now gone, not just on this line but along many others, that it ought to be listed.

When the goods shed ceased to be used, it was taken over by Paper Potts Ltd and is now occupied as a trade warehouse, with the Book 2 Wood business specialising in old pine furniture.

The up platform was 240ft in length, whilst the down platform was 300ft in length, but both were extended in June 1887. Access to the down platform is no longer by a foot crossing between the platforms, but by a path from the level crossing. A waiting room was constructed (presumably on the down platform) for £170 in 1894. A station master's house was added in 1897-8 for £450.

A nearby hotel has been constructed in a railway design, with a semaphore signal as a prop. Where the tracks used to go towards the goods shed, a piece of rail with a buffer stop has been erected for show!

As at Rucking Crossing near Ham Street, a super-gun, for

Appledore's up platform, 25th April 1947. Photo: H C Casserley

firing shells across the English Channel, was put here on a reinforced siding during 1941-2.

Part 1 [page 18] explored how Appledore unexpectedly had its hourly train service taken away in November 2005. However, a short but focused local campaign happily saw a full service restored. Alerted to the clear risk that such cuts might happen again though, parish publications and notices continue to make appeals to residents to keep using the station and ensure its safe continuation.

Like elsewhere, the SER decided to help stage an illegal prize fight near Appledore on 29th January 1856, between Harry

Poulson and Tom Sayers, as the line passed through such a thinly populated area that there was no law enforcement around to stop it. Sayers nearly missed the special train for the fight at 6pm from London Bridge, but went on to win, the SER making £1,000 out of the day. A Kent magistrate accused the SER of aiding and abetting a breach of the peace. The SER, of course, claimed they didn't know what their special train was being arranged for!

Rye Station

The swing bridge was 112 ft long and weighed 116 tons. Its axle for turning was in the centre of the bridge, taking two and a half minutes to turn, enabling boats to pass either side of it when open. A spur and beville-wheels were operated by two men in order to move it. In September 1880, the Rye residents requested the Rother swing bridge be replaced by a permanent static bridge. The SER did not immediately act on this request, no doubt influenced by discovering that the residents hoped to have the replacement rail bridge accommodate a new road. Instead, the SER applied (in a Bill to Parliament) for permission to have its legal responsibility to maintain Rother Bridge dropped. It had been built to take only a single track so as to help boats navigate the bridge, yet it was a double track fixed span bridge. However, in 1902 the SER decided to

Up train bound for Ashford at Rye Station, 1950s. (Lens of Sutton collection)

replace it with an iron (rather than steel!) bridge, which was completed in 1903.

Two level crossings are located at either end of the station, which East Sussex County Council complained about in 1903, as the crossings held up the new invention of the car. A coal stage was constructed in 1854. In May 1873, a boy was killed at Rye. The platforms are staggered (not opposite each other) and an extra platform shelter was added in 1895. A second signal box existed beside the south crossing, whilst the surviving 30-lever signal box opposite the down platform was built in 1893, controlling the block section between Ore and Appledore. The station used to receive custom from the local cattle market located opposite the up platform, separated by the tracks and cattle pens. Sidings were laid in 1874 and two years later one was provided for the business Messrs Kelly. The goods yard shed, built in a grand manner like the station building, closed in 1963 and was demolished in 1984. A wagon turntable and weighbridge once existed at the north end of the station. The footbridge was erected in preparation for proposed electrification of the line in the early 1960s - which never happened.

The jewel in the crown of the Rye line is William Tress' Italianate station building (very good for modelling), which includes loggia columns. The central section of the building, having three bays, has an arcade recessed into the structure. Each of the three sections of the frontage is divided by rusticated pilasters. The elevation of the central roof section is quite unusual (but still modelable). A parcels office was added on the north side of Tress' building by the Southern Railway to replace a lean-to structure. It is now used by a café called The Fat Controller (as the character is called in the *Thomas The Tank Engine* stories).

There are even tales of eight ghosts at nearby inns and along roads in Rye. Some of these appear to interact with the living, as at the White Vine House hotel, where a customer

ABOVE: Rye Station, 2007. BELOW: Rye, 1991. Photos: Paul O'Callaghan

was spoken to by a ghost! Meanwhile, at the Lamb Inn, it is said that poltergeist activity occurs.

Winchelsea Station

No sooner had Winchelsea opened with the line, than the station was closed from 1st September 1851 (just six months later)! A nearby tollgate was discouraging people from accessing the station, so the Mayor of Winchelsea launched a campaign to get it reopened and started negotiations

Winchelsea Station's down platform, when still in use with the station building, 1950s. Note the signal box. (Lens of Sutton Collection).

Loco 31037 at Winchelsea, 21st September 1950. Photo: R C Riley

about the tollgate with a local landowner. The SER agreed on 4th December to reopen it (which is believed to have happened on 1st January 1852). Winchelsea has only a single surviving platform, the Italianate-style old station house designed by William Tress, with bowl eaves, located on the disused down platform. It has a low pitched roof and a veranda platform with a slate-roofed red painted canopy, which extends around the south side of the building and above the public entrance on the west side (although it doesn't go around the wider station house part of the structure). It was up for sale in 2006 (according to

ABOVE: Thumper Unit 207201 at Winchelsea, with the 10.22 Ashford to Hastings train, 1st August 1995. Photo: John Scrace.   BELOW: 'THWART' protests to passing trains (page 18), 29th September 2007. Photo: John Spencer

the brother of the owner, who I met whilst he videotaped the level crossing). Locals had fought to save the line back in 1969, only to have the track singled in the 1970s for two-thirds of its route.

A signal box (possibly of Saxby and Farmer design, as the wooden cabin resided on a brick base with a window) was at the east end of the old down platform and a crossing keeper's cottage was at the east end of the up platform. After 1969 both the signal box and cottage were demolished and even the up platform iron shelter lost its canopy. In the mid-1970s it was home to a potter. In 1870, between Winchelsea and Hastings, £200 was spent on a platelayers hut by the SER.

Today, all the trees around the station building can still be seen. The station is an unpopular half a mile from the village. The old sea cliffs between Rye and Winchelsea (both constructed upon hills) can be seen from the train as it passes over the former harbour, the sea having since retreated, leaving the River Brede in its place.

Following THWART's victory in reinstating fourteen trains each way per day to Winchelsea, a new group known as the Winchelsea Station Adoption Group was formed by John Spencer (with help from the Sussex Community Rail partnership and Samantha Bryant). The role of this group of twelve volunteers (as two working parties) is to improve the station's appearance by keeping it tidy and adding plants and artwork.

Winchelsea has many quaint weatherboarded houses to attract tourists to its little honeypot of history, and also has four ghosts (ones which are really just images of past events, never interacting with the living). To promote the station further, perhaps it could be promoted as "Winchelsea: change here for ghost hunting" on the station name board and associated literature.

Three Oaks and Doleham

In 1990, Three Oaks and Doleham (as explored in the previous 'Halts' section) were still both able to be arrived at by train. When I visited I had to walk from the Hastings 'East End' of Ore, passing down country lanes, past barking dogs and fields full of rabbits, through Three Oaks to Doleham.

When comparing both stations, I am surprised how Doleham station has survived so long. When I walked down Doleham Hill from the spectacular view of the Brede valley at the top, I passed only a dozen terraced houses with cars, and, outside them, children trying to sell vegetables. Doleham station is at the bottom of the hill in a glade. Across the valley is the oast house of Doleham Farm. In 1889, a siding, on the opposite side of Doleham Hill railway bridge, was laid for the East Sussex Brick Company. Local

Doleham, when it had a down platform, 1950s. (Lens of Sutton collection)

residents requested a public siding, but were offered the use of Doleham Siding for a rent of £15 per year. By 1914, only £14 had been made from its rent!

The siding was used from the 1920s for the arrival by train of coal, which was collected from here by a Sentinel steam wagon. The wagon hauled the coal up past Doleham Farm and down to Brede Bridge where a narrow gauge (18 inch) railway would pull the coal up to the Hastings Corporation's Brede Waterworks (construction having began in 1899), in use until 1935. Barges used to haul the coal from Rye Harbour up the River Brede to Brede Bridge, whereupon cranes would transfer the coal into wagons on two wharfs. A Bagnall steam locomotive would haul the coal wagons north and then westward (joining with a track from the shed), onto the Waterworks where the coal would power the two steam pumps. Originally barges had brought the coal up the Brede to the narrow gauge railway wharfs.

However, the barges could only travel up the Brede for two days every two weeks due to the tide, so Doleham siding and the Sentinel steam wagon were used (the tracks between the wharfs and the shed being closed). Doleham siding closed on 6th February 1961. Today, each month Brede Steam Engine Society holds an open day at the Waterworks.

After the Southern Railway took over the SER lines in 1923, only two trains a day called at the three halts. When British Rail took over from Southern in 1948, most trains missed out at least one of the three halts, depriving passengers from, say, Three Oaks, being unable to alight at Doleham, and passengers boarding at Winchelsea also being unable to alight at Doleham. After many complaints, BR implemented sixteen trains a day calling at all stations.

When the line was singled, the down platform was retained at Three Oaks, whilst at Doleham the up platform was retained (having been replaced by a concrete version by Southern). At Three Oaks, the middle section of its up platform survived, as that was made of concrete, with a sign

ABOVE: An old halt sign still survives on the A28 Westfield to Brede road. BELOW: A modern train whizzes past Doleham Halt, July 2006. Photos: Paul O'Callaghan.

Three Oaks, when it had an up platform, 1950s. (Lens of Sutton collection)

on it informing passengers of the directions of Hastings, Rye and Ashford.

When it comes to Three Oaks, it is surprising that Southern treated the station in the same manner as the other two. Unlike Winchelsea Station, Three Oaks Station is in the village itself, and, unlike Doleham, it serves a significant group of bungalows (some also selling vegetables and fruit outside), an osteopath and the Three Oaks Hotel. Back in 1991, as part of British Rail, Network South East trains stopped here every hour, unlike Doleham and Winchelsea. BR recognised the

difference between it and the other two stations.

On 29th September 2007, as we saw earlier, the local station's action group had hoped trains would stop at Three Oaks and Doleham for the Festival Day, but Southern rejected this. Dozens of locals protested on the platforms as the late morning and lunchtime trains whizzed through. They held banners and placards. If the up track was re-extended and electrified back to Three Oaks' old up platform (and the latter restored, with the track signalled for reversible running), then trains from Brighton and

Three Oaks in July 2006. Photo: Paul O'Callaghan

London terminating at Ore would instead terminate at Three Oaks, not interfering with the Rye trains, being on a separate track. Three Oaks, meanwhile, would have an hour train service to Hastings. As already noted, THWART was successful in re-introducing fourteen trains a day. However, Doleham remains with just two trains a day each way (the first and last trains of the day stop here). Rye councillor (and Doleham resident) Bernadine Fiddimore was puzzled in April 2011 as to why a lot of CCTV cameras (controlled from Southern's Croydon control centre) were added at Doleham, with a new automated help point, when there were only two trains a day each way. The councillor had hoped these installations might signal more trains to stop at Doleham (with perhaps even a hail and ride service), thereby serving students needing to reach college, and two local adults who did not have their own cars. However, Southern did not respond to this.

In another curious ghost-hunting diversion, it is worth mentioning that the bridge over the Brede looks just like an average bridge, but is said to be haunted by Sir Goddard Oxenbridge of Brede Place (which he also haunts), who had a reputation of being a child-eating ogre. The story says that whilst he was drunk, the children of Sussex killed him by sawing him in half with a double-handed wooden saw (no steel weapon could apparently hurt him), cutting him in half. The children of West Sussex took away half his body, leaving the other half in East Sussex, in 1535. Officially, however, Sir Goddard was a pious and friendly man! The story of this ghost at Brede is worth telling as it is not documented in any local ghost books or magazines.

Ore Station

In March 1872, the SER considered building an extra station for the rapidly expanding east end of Hastings: Ore. In July 1872, the SER also made this consideration so as to reduce the gap in a lack of stations between Winchelsea and Hastings (remembering that Snailham, Doleham and Three Oaks would not open until 1907). In December 1877, the SER's engineer objected to a station being built so close to Ore Tunnel's mouth. In May 1880 the SER began buying land around Ore, but it was not until the July of 1886 that the company opted to spend £2,800 in constructing a passenger and goods station. A local landowner offered to pay

Entrance to Ore, July 2006.
Photo: Paul O'Callaghan

Ore station, 1950s. Just behind the station to the left, the roof of the EMU shed can be seen. (Lens of Sutton collection)

Five carriage sidings were laid to the west of the station, and just beyond them were cattle pens and the long westward curving siding of 1905 for the Hastings Tramway. The carriage sidings were replaced by a shed for electric trains (covering four tracks) by the Southern Railway in 1935 when the line from Brighton was electrified (it is because the shed was here that the line was electrified beyond Hastings to Ore). A train used to enter the shed every hour from London in the 1980s, and have 27 minutes to be tidied up before being sent back out again.

South of Three Oaks towards Ore, the rail bridge over Eight Acre Lane is one of the few bridges which crosses a road along the line. Photo: Paul O'Callaghan

£1,000 towards costs, but when that was not forthcoming the SER delayed opening until an agreement between them was reached. This agreement was finally made on 17th December 1887, and the station then opened on New Years Day 1888. In 1896 plans were produced to improve Ore station.

In November 1909 a passenger was killed when they looked out of the window in the tunnel. The subsequent Inquest jury ruled that bars should be put on the windows. Ore Tunnel has one air shaft.

Unit 1001 with the 11.11 Hastings to Ashford service at Ore Station, 6th September 1969. The EMU shed roof is more visible here. Photo: John Scrace

A signal box with sliding windows was located to the north of the station, up side, so as to control access to the shed, until 30th January 1977, when Hastings signal box took over Ore box's responsibilities.

Ore station building was on the up platform. It was a standard cheap SER design building of Kentish vernacular clap/weather horizontal boarding (like that still visible at Pluckley), with a shallow pitched roof of slate. It had a platform canopy until around 1983, but this had been removed by 1985. It was built on a low brick base and its chimneys were reduced in height. In May 1986, Ore EMU (Electric Multiple Unit) Shed closed. Today the station building is gone.

To the north of Ore, on the west side, a siding led southwards into a brick works, whilst further north a siding served a power station of the Hastings Corporation Electricity works, where wagons of coal would be taken to be shunted by rope onto a piece of track which lifted up on one side (whilst the wagons were chained to the track), enabling them to tip their load into a hopper to power the electricity works. The works went over to oil firing in the 1960s, and closed in the 1970s, to be succeeded by a gas turbine station.

Hastings' First Station

The first station was constructed in the shape of a 'V' on its side, pointing west. This was built on soil dug out from the tunnels either side of the station. The top half of the V, was the SER platform (Platform 1) for trains to and from Ashford and Tunbridge Wells. In front of the platform were five tracks and then the engine shed, which was built in 1852 and closed in 1929. The goods shed stood beside the SER platform on its south side, at the east end of the station. The southern half of the V-shaped station was the bay platform for the LBSCR (which was blocked off in the Bo-Peep battle

Hastings' original station, 1910. The Ashford platform is on the left (with the goods shed at the end), and the London platforms are on the right. The signal box can be seen in the foreground. (Lens of Sutton collection)

- see the earlier section). Each of these two original platforms had a two-storey building and there was another single storey structure at the merging point of the V.

In October 1869 the SER bought more land for the station and added a turntable. In 1875, the SER added a parcels office for £120 and a new goods station for £4,800 in 1875-6, followed by a new goods office for £300 in 1891. However, the SER did not do anything to improve the room for passengers, who experienced a crush of people when

excursion trains were arriving and departing. A passenger accident on 29th July 1876 was blamed on this. After complaining to the Railway Commission in September 1877, it was only due to legal action by the Hastings Corporation (who made their complaints when they also complained about Warrior Square) that improvements were carried out. Yet *still* the Railway Commissioners had to tell the SER to carry out improvements, in January 1886.

An unusual view of Hastings Station being rebuilt, 1930. The old buildings can be seen to the left (behind the goods shed), whilst the new (current) platforms and footbridge are being constructed. (Lens of Sutton collection)

By 1899, an extra terminal island platform had been built opposite the bay platform serving two tracks either side. It lacked any canopy, so it is believed it was used for excursion traffic. It appears the complaints eventually paid off. The station was re-signalled in 1891 and the platforms improved; until then the station could not cope with trains going to Tunbridge Wells and Ashford at once. In April 1913, the SE&CR closed two local public foot crossings and replaced them with a subway. To the west of the station was the SER signal box.

Bishop Kennet was the station master from November 1852 until March 1877, when he moved to Warrior Square. When he was a boy he had helped his father operate the horse-drawn coach from Maidstone to London. He had also worked at Battle when that station opened.

Hastings' Second Station

Before reconstruction took place, the Southern Railway constructed a turntable at the mouth of Hastings Tunnel, which was used from 1926 to 1957.

In 1931, the Southern Railway opted to reconstruct Hastings Station as two island platforms serving four through tracks, so as to enable its new electric trains to go on through Hastings to the new electric train shed at Ore. Whilst the goods shed survived the rebuild, the engine shed

ABOVE: Hastings, 20th June 1958. The 8.38 train to Ashford is on the left, whilst an EMU train sits to the right, 1958. Photo: H C Casserley BELOW: The Queens Road bridge at Hastings, July 2006. Photo: Paul O'Callaghan.

ABOVE: The 1931 Hastings Station in its 60th year, 1991.
BELOW: The new Hastings station in 2008. Photos: Paul O'Callaghan.

was demolished, replaced by the northern island platform (still used today for Charing Cross trains). All four tracks were signalled for reversible operation for the trains. The new station building was neo-Georgian in style, and linked to the platforms by a footbridge. An inspection pit (dug between the rails to enable staff to look at the underneath of a train) lay to the west of the station.

In 1986, the west end of the track serving Platform 4 (the southernmost platform) was lifted and replaced by a walkway linking the station building on the ground with the southern island platform (Platforms 1 and 2). So Platform 1 became a bay platform, the trains to and from Ashford using it until November 2005. In 2004 the station building was replaced, the new one being closer to Platforms 1 and 2, so shortening the walkway, which is a permanent structure. An old signal box remains, controlling the semaphore signals at the east end of the station.

Before leaving Hastings, mention should be made that a narrow gauge railway was laid to help construct the harbour in 1896.

St Leonards Warrior Square Station

First known as Gensing (named after the local road, which is now Kings Road) until 5th December 1870, in August 1855 the SER decided to improve Warrior Square by

St Leonards Warrior Square Station in summer 1996, before its wall, carrying the name, was demolished. Photo: Paul O'Callaghan.

access road and, in 1878, it announced plans to roof and widen the footbridge. At the time, 210,000 people used the station annually. However, in January 1880, the Railway Commissioners still had to officially order the SER to improve Warrior Square.

The station once had two fine long canopies on both platforms, but under British Rail these were both demolished by 1984, a small cheap box structure replacing the down platform canopy, and with a plain canopy placed on the up side [see photo, page 12]. The station was refurbished in 1999, when £775,000 was spent improving lighting, security, and facilities by Connex, the Hastings Regeneration Partnership and the Railway Heritage Trust.

Unit 5632, with the 11.34 Brighton to Ore train, passes over Bo-Peep Junction on 5th September 1975, with West St Leonards on the right. Photo: John Scrace

spending £270. However, the SER then decided to extend the up (south) side for £680. By 1862, £1,000 had been spent improving the station, and it was again improved in 1864 for £525.

It was later planned to extend just the up platform, but the BoT inspector, Captain Tyler, advised against this. So the SER constructed a footbridge and extended both platforms, but the down platform extension was not completed until 1874.

In 1877, the Hastings Corporation complained to the Railway Commission about Warrior Square, describing the access road as dangerous and calling for the footbridge to be roofed. This prompted the SER to agree to improve the

St Leonards West Marina

Today, if anyone walks up from the seafront to St Leonards West Station on the Tunbridge Wells line, they have to pass over the Bexhill line. When crossing over, if they look west from the bridge, they will see three tracks going westwards, two of which then separate and go either side of an old ruined platform. This was the island platform of the old St Leonards West Marina station, where the steam rail motors from Eastbourne terminated. The station only received its name on 5th December 1870. Either the temporary or permanent station was built by contractor Joshua Davey for £1,997.

Loco shed at St Leonards West Marina, with an R1 class 0-6-07 pulling a 'dead' school's class, 4-4-0 30903 'Charterhouse', on 17th April 1956.
Photo: Norman Simmons

Looking east along the eastbound platform at St Leonards West Marina, 17th April 1956. Photo: Norman Simmons

When complete, the station consisted of two platforms, the southern up platform having the station building upon it, which was the same design as London Road station in Brighton (a two storey building), with single storey wings on either side. This was not constructed until 1888-9.

On the north side of the station stood the engine shed, built around 1889, covering four tracks, whilst in the north east corner of the station was the turntable. To the west of the engine shed, constructed in 1958, was the carriage-washing machine. The original engine shed had only covered two tracks. Steam locomotives continued to use the shed even

St Leonards West Marina, 17th April 1956. Photo: Norman Simmons

after the 1935 electrification of the line (electric trains were served by the shed at Ore).

Despite being right next door to St Leonards West Station, with the quicker service to London, Marina Station remained open beyond the opening of the line to Hastings, as the LBSCR wanted to retain a station of its own in the Hastings district (their line ended at Bo-Peep Junction). However, due to its location on the edge of St Leonards, and competition from West St Leonards, Marina Station

closed on 10th June 1967. Housing now stands where the station building once was.

St Leonards Depot

West of the Marina station, the Bexhill line passes between two railway train sheds and the sea. The first shed is a 750ft cleaning and berthing shed, covering five tracks, with a washing plant (for trains) at its south east end. The second shed is 440ft long and is for maintenance and inspection of trains, having been built in 1956-7 for covering four tracks.

A/X class 0-6-0T 32636 shunting wagons at St Leonards West Marina, 17th April 1956. Photo: Norman Simmons

Train sheds besides the sea at Bulverhythe, with Glyne Gap further west, 2007. A South Eastern train sits in a siding. Photo: Paul O'Callaghan

Glyne Gap Halt

This was one and a quarter miles east of Bexhill, where the A259 met with the coast. It was short and wooden with a few oil lamps, but due to competition from the nearby Bexhill tramway it closed on 1st October 1915. In recent years it has been proposed by a local Bexhill passenger group that the halt could be reopened, as part of a regeneration project, but for now it is concentrating on keeping the London train service to and from Bexhill running. This was one of a series of halts, as described on page 48.

Bexhill Station

The original Bexhill Station was built where the car park now is today. It was the size of Winchelsea Station. A signal box (more like a shed) stood at the east end of the down platform, where the station building was located. Beyond that lay the cattle pens and a goods shed. The up platform was opposite.

This station was replaced in 1891, and then replaced yet again by the present one in 1901. The station was rebuilt in response to the growing population and the opening in 1902 of the Bexhill West Branch Line (the station building for which still survives in Terminus Road; Peter A Harding has written an excellent history of it). The 1901 main station building is on the road above the tracks, and utilises a rectangular lantern-shaped roof (which Eastbourne and Lewes also have), due to the then growing popularity of allowing more light into buildings.

The signal box (which still survives) is located at the west end of the down platform, and beyond that was the goods yard (now the car park). Lavish canopies extended along the platforms (the high point of the platform canopy era was the 1880s and 1890s). Semaphore signals are still used east and west of the station!

At the now rare sloping passenger ramps (linking the platforms with the station building above the tracks), a

Bexhill Station with its lantern roof, 10th September 1996. Photo: John Scrace

people of Bexhill. The Earl's wife's grandfather was the railway contractor, Thomas Brassey.

The station was renamed Bexhill Central from 9th July 1923 (the year the Southern Railway took over) until the Bexhill West branch shut on 16th June 1964.

In 1967, the firm of Stillman & Eastwick–Field published a report on the redevelopment of Bexhill, which they proposed would have a multi-storey car park and office block above the railway line to link Station Road and Devonshire Square. It was not implemented. In recent years the local

Bexhill up platform, with a 4CEP slam-door train in Network SouthEast livery, 2002. Photo: Paul O'Callaghan

separate ramp was constructed for parcels going onto the down platform. In one rail book, there is even a picture of the Gentlemen's urinals here! The station was finished for opening on 30th June 1902.

However, the local landowner, the Eighth Earl De La Warr, objected to the site of the rebuilt station. It was originally proposed (in a 1900 plan) to be built where Sutton Place now is - which meant it would have been close to the Earl's estate, but would not have been very good for the working

ABOVE: Bexhill signal box, 5th September 1975. BELOW: Unit 207202 with the 13.54 Ashford to Eastbourne train. Photos: John Scrace

preservation society successfully had the station Grade 2 listed, preventing its replacement.

During 2006, Bexhill's station canopies were re-roofed.

The Railmotor Halts (Collington, Cooden Beach, Normans Bay, Pevensey Bay and Stone Cross)

The Eastbourne Branch, using the spur link line from Willingdon Junction to Stone Cross Junction, was selected to be part of a new type of train service between Eastbourne and St Leonards West Marina (the South Eastern & Chatham Railway operated the line eastwards to Hastings and objected to the new service going through to Hastings as it would interfere with their trains from Tunbridge Wells). The new railmotor service was the LBSCR reaction to the creation of tramways around its network (which included south London) and, from 1903, the introduction of motor buses on the roads. The railway companies of Britain had noticed that people were using the new motor buses and trams, even though the passengers were willing to wait without even shelter, forgoing the services of a station. This meant that railways could construct very cheap stations to compete with the tram and bus services. Thus the LBSCR, like other railway companies, opted to use a steam railcar (earlier experiments with which had been disappointing), but now in conjunction with a new type of station: the halt.

The typical halt was cost efficient in that it was a short wooden platform of 70ft for a single carriage train to stop at, some platforms not even having a shelter, and no staff. Due to their small size, it meant the halts could be erected where there was little room for a full-sized station, and could therefore be spaced close together to compete with the tram and bus stops. If the halt lacked lighting and was not next to a level crossing, then it was deemed too unsafe to be open after dark and so was closed at that time. Being so cheap to construct justified the railway companies taking a chance with a station at places deemed too small (e.g. hamlets) to justify the expense of a full-sized station in the past.

Many of these halts have closed since the 1960s (although some shut even as early as 1915), whilst others have become stations. In the Eastbourne area there were three halts, of which only one, on the edge of Eastbourne borough, has been closed. The railmotor (or railcar), meanwhile, was the first train service to integrate the drivers' cab and engine with the passenger carriage – in other words, just like the front carriage of a modern Electric Multiple Unit, but steam and petrol powered. The LBSCR purchased two Dick Kerr four-wheel petrol railcars, which were claimed to go as fast as 55mph. However, these vehicles could not cope with the passenger levels and were subsequently replaced by two steam railcars (the petrol vehicles being sent to work

the Kemp Town Branch in Brighton). The vehicles were all third class, and could carry up to 48 people (as described on pages 14-18 in Part 1).

On the wet day of 14th September 1905, the Railmotor service began operating to six halts between St Leonards West Marina and Eastbourne, two of which have now closed. The halts, however, officially opened on 11th September, three days earlier. In the Eastbourne area, the halts were at Stone Cross, Pevensey Bay and Normans Bay. There were initially six trains each way, per day. In 1910 these were reduced to three trains, with a fourth train operating between just Eastbourne and Pevensey (serving only the Eastbourne area). Bell punch tickets were issued by the guard on the train. The LBSCR ceased using their two steam railmotors in 1911, having lost faith in them. The railmotors were replaced by a steam locomotive and two carriages, known as push-pull trains, which enabled the driver to operate the train from either end and did not require the locomotive to be turned around on a turntable or run around its carriages. Such trains operated on branch lines until the 1960s. The Eastbourne line was electrified in 1935, providing a half-hourly train service between Brighton and Ore.

Collington Wood Halt

This halt, three-quarters of a mile west of Bexhill, was

Collington in 1999. Photo: Paul O'Callaghan

system of Bexhill. Despite having a signal box by 1921, this was only ever called Cooden (though this or Norman's Bay may once have been called Pevensey Sluice – see below). It was the Southern Railway who rebuilt Cooden Beach into a proper station in 1935 (although completion may not have happened until 1937), with concrete platforms, full lighting, shelters and, on the up side at ground level (the platforms and tracks are high up), the station building. Today, passengers using the platforms have to pass through a shop, as that is what the building has become! The station never had goods facilities. Cooden Beach Station marks the

Cooden Beach, October 2005. Photo: Paul O'Callaghan

closed after only a year, on 1st September 1906, but was then reopened on 1st June 1911 as West Bexhill Halt. Then, in 1929, it was renamed Collington Halt. The 'Halt' bit of the name was removed in 1970. The Braggs Lane footbridge at Collington was erected in 1921.

Cooden Beach

Two and a quarter miles west of Bexhill, this opened as Cooden Golf Halt, was renamed Cooden Halt, and then, on 7th July 1935, was renamed Cooden Beach Station. To the south of the halt lay the terminus point of the tramway end of the suburbs of Bexhill and the beginning of Cooden Golf Course and the adjoining area of reclaimed land. In recent years it underwent refurbishment, costing half a million pounds.

Normans Bay

It is disputed in books as to whether this halt once carried a different name, as this also is reported to have been called Pevensey Sluice (the name of the local village until the station opened). It retained its wooden platforms and oil-lit lamps until 1934. It is located on the east side of Havensmouth private level crossing (the road is private, but used by public cars). A crossing keeper's house once stood beside the level crossing, on the north side of the crossing, east of the road. This was gone by 1992. In 2005, the remaining crossing keeper's hut (opposite the site of the house) was staffed by a man called Jim (who mistook your author for a local press journalist/photographer, as Jim had been trying to get the station's centenary marked.) A colleague of Jim's reported that the halt had either been opened as a result of people visiting a beached whale, or that the event had at least helped to prevent the station from closing. The ticket office was not erected until after electrification in 1935.

Normans Bay serves a small village, which includes caravans in the summer, a converted Martello Tower, a

ABOVE: Loco 1060 at Normans Bay with the Lewes to Ore train, 22nd October 1939. Photo: H C Casserley. BELOW: Normans Bay crossing, with Jim the crossing keeper, 15th October 2005. Photo: Paul O'Callaghan

bright pink house (which passengers on trains always seem to talk about and like), and the Star Inn. Originally this was a sluice keeper's cottage at the beginning of the 15th century, when the marshes were drained for sheep grazing. Built in 1402, it was called The Sluice House. It went on to become the Star of Bethlehem Inn, used by smugglers for centuries. It has now been extended into a restaurant and is well worth a visit.

At the end of the nineteenth century, the sea wall (embankment) collapsed during a storm, letting seawater flood all around the Star Inn, forcing the landlord to retreat upstairs with his pigs and sheep!

Train departing Normans Bay, 29th October 2006. Photo: Paul O'Callaghan

To the north east of the inn lies the site of the long-lost village of Northye, the chapel of which was called St James, which Normans Bay's church was named after when the Duke of Devonshire gave the land for it. There was a shop there called Alice's around 1940.

Pevensey Bay

This halt is two miles east of Pevensey and Westham station, beside the main A259 road. Pevensey Bay Halt, which has also had concrete platforms replace its wooden platforms, once had a level crossing keeper's box on the east side of the crossing. Its name, Wallsend Crossing, pre-dated the box.

Pevensey Bay crossing, June 1974. Photo: Roger Quantrill

The keeper's box at Pevensey Bay crossing, June 1976. Photo: Roger Quantrill

Automatic lifting barriers were installed in 1974 and, in May 1976, the signal box at Pevensey and Westham station took remote control of Wallsend, before the Wallsend box was then demolished. This halt today has the least number of trains stopping at it, so its future does not look good. From 1877 until the 1970s, a footbridge once spanned the line here for use when the gates were shut, on the west side of the crossing. A horse and carriage would collect people from here and take them to the Bay Hotel.

Pevensey and Westham Station

The station was rebuilt in 1892-3 due to a continuous stream of complaints from locals about its condition. The station had its goods shed and cattle pens on the north side, with the signal box (still surviving at the east end of the down platform, beside the level crossing). The goods yard closed in 1961. During World War II, station staff and track workers formed a nightwatch group to look out for German invaders. The waiting shelter on the up platform was a small building, with the station master's house beyond that. Barriers were installed on the crossing from 1975. Local history author Colin J Huggett (whose great grandfather worked as crossing keeper at Pevensey Bay) saved the wheel from Pevensey and Westham signal box, when the latter was upgraded to control-lifting barriers, making the wheel (for turning to lower the old gates) redundant. The up platform has a bus-type shelter on it, but the station building survives, featuring some historic railway pictures of the station, as if someone is trying to make it into a museum.

In 1992, the iron up semaphore signal was replaced by a steel one. The iron one was obtained by the neighbouring school, and can still be seen from passing trains. When the signal points up, this lets the children know it's dry enough to play on the playing field!

In Mr Huggett's book, *Under The Eagle*, he tells local stories

Pevensey and Westham signal box, 1970. Photo: Roger Quantrill

of local people, so if you want to hear what happened when a horse bolted at the sound of a signal arm being lowered, or about the railway ganger who had a detonator put down his plate layer's hut chimney, or an event (like that in the Ealing comedy film *The Titfield Thunderbolt*) of the Stone Cross signal man shooting rabbits, I suggest you read his book.

Stone Cross Halt

This was one and a half miles from Hampden Park Station,

and located beside the bridge over the old Hailsham to Eastbourne road. It did manage to have its platforms replaced by concrete before it was closed on 7th July 1935. Due to the massive amount of housing development over the past two decades, particularly at Langney, if Stone Cross were reopened as Stone Cross and Langney, it could have as many passengers as Cooden.

Stone Cross Junction signal box received oil for its lamps, along with water and coal, from a guards' van on a train, as no road led to the box. Roger Quantrill has some interesting memories regarding signalling at Stone Cross:

"I remember one Sunday afternoon having Billy Smart's Circus train standing on the down branch home signal for a while. I think it was to Hastings; that was the last one as far as I can remember, about 1963-4. That [was a] hard winter, trying to switch out the signal box, which involved setting the road [track] up the main [to Polegate]: I swept the snow out of the points and by the time I had got back in the box to pull the points [by the box levers] they [the points] were full of snow. I tried again and failed, so next time I put some cotton waste soaked in paraffin and lit it under the bolts - and the snow still beat me! So I had to stay in all night, this at 2am.

We never had a train for three days; then, a big steam loco with a snow plough on it [arrived]. Stone Cross road bridge

ABOVE: Loco 2053, with the 9.52 train from Brighton to Ashford, at Stone Cross, 9th September 1933. Photo: H C Casserley   BELOW: Inside Stone Cross signal box, with Roger Quantrill at the levers.

was full of snow to the top. I had a little cream Reliant van under there – we didn't see it for three weeks!"

Hampden Park Station

As with the Three Oaks area, local people had to campaign to get their local station of Willingdon to open, which it did on 1st January 1888. When the local landowner, Lord Hampden, began turning his land into residential development around the station, it was renamed Hampden Park on 1st July 1903. It had a goods yard on its west side, accessed from the south, which lasted until 30th November 1964. An extra siding was laid in 1910. The station is constructed of clap/weatherboarded material, of which around only a dozen examples exist. The signal box, like Eastbourne's, still exists, and controls the level crossing (the gates being replaced by barriers on 5th April 1976, when the box gained a flat-roofed extension on its north side).

Until June 1930, half a mile to the north, another signal box controlled Willingdon Junction, where the Eastbourne branch meets the 1871 spur line to Pevensey and Westham. After June 1930, Hampden Park signal box controlled the junction. Semaphore signals are still used at this junction.

Eastbourne's Second Engine Shed

The double-track Eastbourne branch, now part of the main

line, continues heading almost south across the Eastbourne-Willingdon Levels, and today passes a miniature gauge railway on the east side. Beyond that, the suburb of Roselands and a local school arises, whilst on the right is some rough ground where wandering foxes can often be spotted. This rough ground was Eastbourne's second engine shed, for servicing steam and diesel locomotives, from 1911 until 1968. The site had originally been earmarked for carriage works, but local opposition forced the London, Brighton & South

Eastbourne's second engine shed, with locos 30533, 0131891 and Stan 4-80095, 16th September 1961. Photo: Roger Haggar

Coast Railway company to construct the carriage works at Lancing. Instead they built the engine shed here. It ran parallel to the branch, and had seven tracks passing through it, joining the branch at the south end, and converging to a turntable at the north end. At this end of the engine shed, a towering structure was erected over the No. 1 shed track in 1929. This was part of an experiment to supply pulverised coal to the U-Class steam locomotive A629, which had been adapted for this special coal. However, the locomotive suffered an explosion in 1932, thus stopping the trial. The explosion caused black coal dust to fall on Eastbourne, sparking complaints. The locomotive was fixed and carried on until 1962, when it was sent to Canada. After 1935, the inspection pits and smoke ducts were removed from tracks four to seven. During World War II, bombing wrecked the roof, so what was left was removed, although some re-roofing had occurred by 1950. However, by the time the shed closed the roof was completely gone (see photo, left). The shed ceased servicing steam locomotives in June 1965, as the era of steam locomotives was drawing to a close. The engine shed switched to servicing diesel locomotives until 1968, before being demolished in 1969.

At the south end of the engine shed, where the shed track joined the Eastbourne branch, the Crumbles Branch Line swung in from the east to run parallel to it until 1967. The

Eastbourne branch's double tracks, and the single track of the Crumbles branch then passed the old waterworks on the west side, whilst on the east side two sidings swung in from the north east. The first of these was Banbridges & Shell's joint siding, with their business yard at the end being where Gosdon's removals business is now based today. The second siding served the timber yard of Davy & Mannington and also the business of Lunsford. Both sidings joined the Crumbles branch. This siding's track point was switched with an Annetts' patent lock, the key being attached to the train staff baton. After this, both the Eastbourne and Crumbles branch tracks pass beneath Whitley Road bridge, and begin to turn south westward. South of Whitley Road bridge, on the east side, was a large coal yard with plenty of sidings, connecting with the branch. The coal sidings closed in May 1983. On the west side were an array of carriage sidings, which are still located from here southwards today. Although the sidings are much reduced since 1983, a train washing plant still survives here.

On approach to Eastbourne station, the siding from the Duke of Devonshire's estate yard swung in from the north east, with a gate across it like the other sidings. This estate yard was important in the development of Eastbourne and was one of the reasons for the Crumbles branch's existence. In 1910, the siding reached its buffer behind Winter

The train washing plant at Eastbourne. The coal yard was once to the right of this site. Photo: Paul O'Callaghan

Road, next to a smithy. A separate bridge was constructed so that Cavendish Road could pass over the siding. The yard was used for the arrival of shingle, brought from the Crumbles, which would then be used in the construction of Eastbourne's buildings. The siding took twenty wagons. By 1948 this siding was gone. At the point where the estate yard siding joined the Eastbourne branch, another short siding went straight ahead directly opposite (the Eastbourne

Ivatt 2MT 41326 loco at Eastbourne's second engine shed, 1963. Photo: Roger Haggar

Branch swinging right to the station). This short siding served Carrara Wharf for the monument masons R Frances & Sons. The Crumbles branch meanwhile, joined the Eastbourne branch as it passed beneath Cavendish road.

Eastbourne's First Engine Shed

Further along, but on the west side, was the first engine shed for Eastbourne, shaped like a half of a semi-circle, with a turntable in front of it. The eight tracks which entered the shed were accessed from the Eastbourne branch by way of

the turntable. In 1911, this engine shed was closed due to the lack of room for expanding the shed and because the site could be put to other railway purposes. This was why the second engine shed was built half a mile away.

Eastbourne Station

The first station building was 20ft by 12ft and was located where the Royal Mail sorting office now is, south west of the present station, thus causing the curve of the branch into the station to be tighter. It was decided to reconstruct the station at the present location due to the lack of room

Signal box at Eastbourne, 10th July 1976. Photo: John Scrace

for expansion on the original site. The first station building (described by one person as a wooden shack) was moved to the west side of the goods yard to become 1 Wharf Road, and was used by railway families before becoming a furniture store in the 1950s. In 1961 it was used as a builder's store. The first engine shed had two tracks, and was located west of the goods shed. Two long buildings were erected opposite each other with space in-between.

The temporary second station was opened in 1866, on the site of the former arrival platform of the original. This was converted into a refreshment room in 1872 when the station was adapted and reopened (some call this the third station), before being enlarged and rebuilt in 1886 (which some people regard as the fourth station). A new signalling system, based on those at Brighton and London Bridge, was installed at the same time. The current station buildings date from the 1886 rebuild, which gave it the distinctive lantern roof and vaulted canopy on the east side. The rebuild design is referred to, somewhat inappropriately, as Brighton Baroque (!), built by F D Bannister of the London Brighton & South Coast Railway.

Opposite Eastbourne's first engine shed site is the 72-lever signal box, which amazingly still survives, yet is not listed!

Like other stations, Eastbourne had a steam crane and cattle pens, the latter located between the passenger station

ABOVE: Eastbourne Station, October 2005. Photo: Paul O'Callaghan
BELOW: Eastbourne Station concourse, c. 1900 (author's collection)

ABOVE: Looking south at Eastbourne, 1897. (Bob Cookson collection)
BELOW: The same view in 2005. Photo: Paul O'Callaghan

and goods shed (which has now been converted into a shopping centre). In June 1951, a railway exhibition was held to promote the modernisation of the line. On 25th August 1958, a train from Glasgow hit the train from Ore to London Bridge, killing five people and injuring 25.

The station had four platforms, the one for tracks 3 and 4 being wide enough to take a cab road along it. At its far end, a photograph has revealed a short track indenting into the wide platform for short freight traffic, possibly postal trains. On 12th April 1977, the siding beside Platform 4's track was taken out of use, whilst its main track was reduced in length, and the wide canopy reduced in width, so as to enable a new ring road to be laid. Platform 4 has since closed completely. This hasn't stopped station screens listing departures from Platform 4 in recent years! The weather vane upon the clock is a relatively modern donation by the Eastbourne Society. During World War II the German Luftwaffe (air force) bombed Eastbourne Station in 1942. On 10th September 1942, two staff practicing how to use a fire pump were killed. As Eastbourne was on the coast, and closer, therefore, to the German air fields, it was often too late to sound the air raid siren. In 1943 a bomb fell between Platforms 3 and 4, breaking the tracks.

Eastbourne Station was listed on 3rd July 1981. It is yellow brick in construction, with red brick dressings and slate roofs in a combined Feneland Italina style, with two fronts and a large clock tower with a sharp pyramid roof on the corner. To the left there is a large semi-domed French pavilion roof with fish scale tiles and iron cresting. To the right stands a rectangular hall with an arcaded upper storey and wooden lantern. The iron and glass canopies are largely retained on the outside, but the concourse roof has been replaced in steel. 1930's Southern Railway extension to the left is rendered in a contemporary style.

Polegate Station

Now we retrace our steps back along the Eastbourne branch, through Hampden Park, to Willingdon Junction. Having previously come down from Ashford on the right-hand tracks at this junction, we now take the left-hand tracks, so staying with the original Eastbourne branch back up to the old main line Hastings to Brighton.

As the branch completes its curves to the west, the original route of the Hastings to Brighton line, which enabled trains to bypass Eastbourne and go straight from Pevensey to Polegate and vice versa (described earlier), can still be seen. Today this short stretch at the west end has some small buildings upon its track bed, and the site of the old junction can also be made out. Immediately after this was the second junction, with the Hailsham branch to Eridge.

ABOVE: Loco B377 at Eastbourne Station, 26th April 1931. Photo: H C Casserley BELOW: 2-Bil units 2099 and 4 Lav 2935 at Eastbourne, 1962. Photo: Roger Haggar

Polegate Station, c. 1960. Photo: R K Blencowe

the Hastings line was east of the first station. When the branch was extended to Eridge, trains through Eridge and Hailsham would go on to Eastbourne, so the junction was moved in 1881 and turned to face east, enabling trains to go to Eastbourne without reversing. A new station was built to replace the first so that trains from Eridge would stop at Polegate. This station was located 300 yards to the east. It also meant that the junction with the Eastbourne Branch had to be moved further eastwards.

The replacement station had three signal boxes: the first at the level crossing (which still survives), one tall grand

Unit 2679, with the 14.12 Ore to Brighton train, approaching Polegate's 'A' signal box, 5th September 1968. Photo: John Scrace

The first station at Polegate was on the site of the current one, beside the village's level crossing. It served a horse-drawn bus carriage to Hailsham and Polegate. The buildings of this first station long survived its closure, not being demolished until the 1960s. They consisted of an original single storey building from 1846, and a two storey extension dating from 1849. The first station later became the goods yard when its replacement opened. An engine shed with a turntable existed on the north side of the railway.

When the branch to Hailsham opened, the junction with

Polegate signal box in 2006. Photo: Paul O'Callaghan

signal box (like the surviving signal box at Eastbourne) at the west end of the station to control the junction with the Eridge line, and the third at the east end, controlling the junction between the branch to Eastbourne and the direct line to Pevensey and Westham (which became an engineers' siding in 1974, and was lifted in 1984).

The station had four platform faces, with two island platforms serving four tracks, all on an embankment. They were linked by a subway to the main building on the north side of the station. An overall roof covering the two middle tracks existed until at least 1875. An old coach body was used as a staff mess room.

After the branch to Eridge was closed beyond Hailsham on 14th June 1965, and then to Hailsham itself on 9th September 1968, the four platform station was no longer required to be so large. On 25th May 1986, the third and present Polegate Station opened. It is located on the site of the first station, history now having come full circle. Its buildings are like those of Eltham Station, another example which replaced two earlier versions, in 1985.

Today the station building of the four platform station has been saved as a restaurant, *The Old Polegate Station*, with a painting of Victorian passengers boarding a steam train as the restaurant (pub style) name board. Much of the line to Eridge (known for many years as the Cuckoo Line) has been converted as far as Heathfield as the Cuckoo Trail, a cycle path. Along it, Hellingly Station building has been the only one to survive, whilst at Horam only the platforms survive. The tunnel beneath Heathfield survives with industrial

Polegate old station (now a restaurant), 2006. Photo: Paul O'Callaghan

buildings in front of it, and is closed off. Maybe one day the rest of the route through the tunnel to Eridge can be converted into the Cuckoo Trail, so rendezvousing with the Spa Valley steam railway. This would be a great day out for any railway buff and their family on bikes.

Beyond Polegate, the railway to Lewes passes over Wilmington level crossing, which used to have a signal box to control it. Today it is controlled by automatic lifting barriers, although sadly, in late 2005, it failed to stop a suicidal woman deliberately parking her car on the tracks so as to be killed by a train (but also putting those on the train at risk). Luckily all passengers survived the impact, but the woman died. A few years earlier, on the Reading to Taunton line, a male driver did the same thing, but in so doing killed five people, including a young girl, when the train hit his car. Many believe that this kind of unfortunate and unpredictable behaviour by suicidal individuals justifies signal persons being brought back to oversee level crossings, being able to halt trains immediately should such events occur. Their presence would surely act as a deterrent.

On a lighter note, passengers passing this area can look south east at the slopes of the South Downs, and see the ancient Long Man of Wilmington, originally created by digging off the grassland of the slope to reveal the chalk underneath.

Berwick Station

After passing over the River Cuck (which becomes the Cuckmere), Berwick Station is reached. It is a little museum piece, with the best little signal box west of Eastbourne, semaphore signalling (as at Polegate), a country station building on the down platform, and the prettiest up platform shelter on the whole route. It is in desperate need of listing. The level crossing is located between the station and the brick signal box with chimney, its lower windows now bricked up. The crossing received lifting barriers in 1963 and a siding was removed in 1964, when goods traffic ceased.

Loco at Berwick Station at the western end of the up platform, 13th June 1962. Photo: R K Blencowe

Berwick signal box, 2006. Photo: Paul O'Callaghan

Berwick Station in 2006. Photo: Paul O'Callaghan

On the down side was the Cuckmere Brick Company's clay and brick pit. Further away, near Berwick Church, was the Ludlow Brick & Tile company (1880-1965), which featured a narrow gauge railway. The works were left to rot until the 1980s. Berwick has no footbridge, with passengers simply using the level crossing.

This station is often featured on local postcards, and is one which most railway buffs would want to visit, as it has changed so little. Thankfully it has the most interesting walks of any station between the Eastbourne and Brighton stations, ideal for a family day out: a short one around the nearby Arlington Reservoir, and a longer one along the country road south to the tourist honeypot village Alfriston, where the South Downs Way can be picked up for a walk up to the Long Man, or the path along the Cuck to Cuckmere Haven, the jewel of the East Sussex coast, where the coastal path from Eastbourne to Seaford can be joined.

To the east of Glynde is the second level crossing at Ripe, which had a signal box from 1899. It was closed in 1965.

Glynde Station

Opened in 1846 with the line, this station only gained most of its buildings in 1874 at a cost of £895. The main structure consists of a long single storey building on the down side (with a triangular doorway canopy on its road side), but has lost its platform canopy. On the up platform, not only is there an old shelter, but a second one exists at the foot of the roofed footbridge steps. A signal box once stood on the down platform (London end). It closed on 1st March 1970. The goods yard was once the hidden home

Glynde in 2005. Photo: Paul O'Callaghan

Glynde Station, with its platform signal box, seen with loco 2471 pulling the 9.22 Hastings to Brighton train, 9th October 1932. Photo: H C Casserley

for 12-inch bore guns during World War II. Between 1943 and 1947, an emergency level crossing existed for soldiers at the east end of the station. The station still retains a station master's house at the west end of the single storey building. In 1968 the road bridge was rebuilt.

To the north west of Glynde Station, a branch trailed away for Newington Lime Works, the works and chalk quarry being at the hill below the prehistoric Mount Caburn. The branch crossed the Glynde Reach (once navigable). Another branch curved away from the station east of it, going northwards to a clay pit, the trees along the track bed marking its route out. To the south east of the station there were two sidings serving Balcombe pit, which had a narrow gauge railway system. Two private sidings went off from the station yard. The station serves a pretty village with a cricket green and quaint café. Up the hill to the north is a farm which hosts llamas, alpacas, and a camel, just before you reach Glyndebourne, the world-famous opera venue. A path from west of here goes up the steep hill to Lewes.

Southerham Junction

After passing over Glynde Reach and the A27 (once via a level crossing, but now over a bridge, which began construction in 2007) the line merges with the branch to Seaford. This is Southerham Junction, three quarters of a mile east of Lewes. The junction had its own signal box of 23 levers until it closed on 18th September 1976 (the surviving signal box at Lewes taking control of the junction). It was then that the junction was moved from the north end of the cutting to the south, so the Seaford tracks no longer ran beside the Eastbourne line. A siding to G Newington & Co. cement works (becoming Lewes Portland Cement Co. by 1910) also used to curve away from here, northwards. In 1929 it was taken over by Eastwards and eventually closed in 1981.

Immediately beyond the old site of Southerham Junction, the line crosses the Ouse River. On 5th April 1935, a

ABOVE/BELOW: Southerham signal box, with Unit 5619 and the 9.54 Brighton to Seaford train passing by, 5th September 1975. Photos: John Scrace

cement barge damaged one of the eight rail bridges' piers, preventing it from being able to be automatically opened to shipping. It took 30 men to open and close the bridge to boats until repairs had been done.

The local gas company in Lewes used to send its gas tanks by barge to Newhaven, and so had a legal right to require the bridge to be opened. When the Southern railway proposed to change Lewes' gas lighting to electric, the gas company blackmailed Southern by stating they would resume sending their gas by barge, so requiring the bridge to be opened for their boats and thus interfering with train services. Consequently, Southern dropped the idea of electric lighting for Lewes Station, which did not receive it until after nationalisation.

Lewes Station

The history of Lewes Station is complicated. The first station was in Friars Walk, opening when the first stage of the line from Brighton went into service in May 1846, before the rest of the line to Hastings (Bulverhythe), which opened just one month later in June 1846. Despite opening the rest of the line only the following month, the company had the first Lewes Station built as a terminus, so the newer line on to Hastings left the earlier line just to the south of Friars Walk. In other words, a train to Hastings would first turn

Lewes, looking east, 4th May 1930. Photo: H C Casserley

left to go into the Friars Walk station, then reverse back out to turn right to go on to Hastings (and vice versa)! - a bit like Inverness today.

The Friars Walk station building consisted of yellow brick and four big Corinthian pilasters with five bays. After it closed it was used as railway offices into the 1960s.

Apparently there had been a promise made to the people of Lewes that they would be consulted on the site of Lewes station, but this did not happen, causing one Lewes tradesman to complain by letter. He also protested about the route of the line not going through St Mary's Lane to Southerham, but instead through the land of a BL&HR

director's land, and raised the issue that the tight curve of the line scared people. He pointed out that the promise of a large station building for passengers, which was supposed to make up for the changes, had not materialised but a "cow shed" had been erected instead (the Friars Walk station).

To the west of Friars Walk, from 1846 until 1848, was the Southover (or Ham) platform (opposite where the present signal box and footbridge are located), for residents of the Southover High Street area. It was accessed by a path from Lansdown Place. There was a proposal to build a spur line

Lewes on 4th September 1953, still clearly showing its long-disused old platforms and the now removed Friars Walk line to the left. Photo: R C Riley

Loco 1215 pulls the 9.25 Brighton to Seaford train at Lewes, 10th October 1932. Photo: H C Casserley

from Friars Walk (the 'cow shed' station) to join the line to Hastings, so trains could run into the station and then branch out again, like they do to reach Hampden Park and Eastbourne today, but this never happened. To complicate matters further, to avoid trains being constantly reversed into and out of Lewes Station, the Pinwell Lane (unroofed) platforms were opened on the Hastings line, just to the west of the junction for Lewes Station from 1847. However, trains continued to go into and out of the Friars Walk station.

A general view of Lewes and its signal box, looking west in September 2005, (with the London line peeling off to the right). Photo: Paul O'Callaghan

The Friars Walk and Pinwell platforms were finally replaced by a new station (the second) in November 1857, at the junction of the Brighton–Hastings and Wivelsfield–Lewes lines. The extra trains from London via Wivelsfield were brought in to serve the Newhaven branch, and the desire to increase boat trains to/from Newhaven and the opening of the branch to Uckfield (from 1858) provided another motive for constructing this new station. This had its engine shed and turntable between the platforms for London and Brighton (in the centre of the V-shaped station). The goods depot was beside the site of Friars Walk Station (east side).

The new station building, also located in the centre of the V-shaped layout, was like a Swiss chalet, having ornate tiles. On the north side of the down platform (for trains to Hastings) was a bay platform, which had the canopy extended right over the track. Meanwhile, the goods shed was beside the up platform (for Brighton) on the south side.

On 24th September 1879, a locomotive blew up on the London-bound up platform, whilst hauling a train to London. A later report found the spring safety valves to be responsible.

In 1868, when the Uckfield line was extended to Tunbridge

The Brighton platforms at Lewes, September 2005. Photo: Paul O'Callaghan

Wells, its junction with the Wivelsfield line west of Lewes was closed and the Uckfield line redirected to join the line from Hastings to the east of Lewes, passing through Friars Walk to reach it.

The current (and third) station was, like the second station, lifted up and moved a little southwards, and turned slightly clockwise. So, rather than the Brighton line passing through Lewes Station from the south west, going north east, and then tightly curving south east, the Brighton line now passed through the station from the west, going eastward. This lessened the previously tight curve of the line sweeping in from Wivelsfield. Whilst this new layout deprived the Brighton line from linking with the old 1857 route of the Wivelsfield line, the latter route and its now redundant 1857 Lewes Station platforms were retained. This route became known as the Goods Loop. Where the new route through the new station joined this old route, there was the East Yard, the junction of 'Lewes East' controlled by a 33-lever signal box. The Goods Loop was disconnected from the new route when the East Yard was shut in June 1970. Today, the disused space where East Yard was can be made out as trains curve westward to enter Lewes Station.

Meanwhile, the 1868 Uckfield line (which was eventually closed in 1968), whilst retaining its link with the Goods Loop, was extended over the Loop's old platform buildings

Lewes Station main building, displaying its lantern roof, September 2005.
Photo: Paul O'Callaghan

to connect with the new route (this reconstruction was undertaken to reduce the aforementioned tight curve of the route from Wivelsfield and the line east of the station). At its zenith, the new (present) station had three platforms serving the London trains and four serving the Brighton trains. The first train to enter the new station was on 17th June 1889. When the platforms were lengthened to take twelve-carriage trains (as part of the Southern Railway's electrification of the lines in 1935), the Goods Loop connection to the new line was shifted nearer the tunnel mouth on the Wivelsfield line and the signal box on the north side was closed, being replaced by another on the south side of the new junction (this box no longer exists). In 1972, the London Loop platform (Platform 1) closed, so Platform 2 became the new Platform 1 (which it remains today).

The London and Brighton platforms are linked by a roofed footbridge. Where it passes behind the station building, there are no windows along its east side, because the roof extends right across the centre area between the Brighton and London platforms. As well as steps linking the footbridge to the present Platform 2, and another set to Platform 3, in the centre of the area between the platforms is a sloping ramp leading up to the footbridge. The station building is constructed of different-coloured bricks with dwarf balustrade. It is topped with a lantern for a roof (like that at Bexhill and the east wing of Eastbourne), as the late Victorians liked a lot of light in their public buildings. Since the mid-1980s, a canopy has been reinstated along the central part of the front of the station building. The station was partly built by Longleys.

The Brighton platforms lost the original 1889 Platforms 4 and 5, which both served the same track, when Platform 6 was extended for longer trains in 1971. Gravel now fills up the track bed for these old platforms, enabling people to walk across at ground level to the new Platform 3 (formerly Platform 6). The footbridge stretches across to serve Platforms 5 and 6 (formerly Platforms 7 and 8).

The junction signal box is still open as a panel box. After a flood from the Ouse in 1960, the borough surveyor wanted to blow up the London platforms so flood water couldn't collect at the west end of the London platforms, but British Railways' district engineer refused permission. In October 2000, Lewes platforms were again flooded - the next train to London replaced by the next canoe! Yes, canoeists were paddling along the flooded tracks, one such image appearing on the front cover of *Private Eye* with a joke caption.

Falmer Station

After leaving Lewes (from the Brighton platforms), the line dives into the 107 yard-long Kingston Tunnel and then afterwards runs past the site of Ashcombe signal box, which existed until 1933, before arriving at Falmer.

The first Falmer Station opened on 6th June 1846, at the eastern mouth of Falmer Tunnel. This closed in 1865, being inconvenient for locals and Stanmer House (mansion), and was replaced by a station just to the west of the tunnel. This in itself was rebuilt in 1890. A private siding existed nearby for coal to be delivered to the water pumping station of the Brighton Corporation. A goods siding existed at the east end (north side) of the station. The goods yard closed

ABOVE: Loco 1737 at Falmer, with the Brighton to Ashford train, 11th October 1933. Photo: H C Casserley BELOW: Falmer, 27th April 1971. Photo: John Scrace

in 1961. The up platform shelter had been replaced by a flat dreary roof structure by 1983. What makes Falmer station appealing to railway enthusiasts is the rare type of surviving signal box. In 1930, the old signal box was closed and the station building extended onto the down platform to accommodate the signal frame. This meant that station staff could now double up as signalmen.

In 1958, the University of Sussex opened its doors to the north of the station, with another next door on the south side. Many students teem on and off the train between here and Brighton. Falmer is a tiny, pretty, village located above Falmer Tunnel, with its houses and church around a pond. Sadly, in 2007, despite local council support, the villagers, already swamped with two universities and the main A27 trunk road, lost the battle to prevent Brighton & Hove Football Club building its new stadium here.

Moulsecoomb Station

Beyond Falmer, a three-arch viaduct carries the line across the main A27 trunk road, which became a dual carriageway in 1967, necessitating the western arch being reinforced with a bow-string span. Moulsecoomb is the newest station on the route, serving the eastern suburb of Brighton and also Brighton Polytechnic, and was opened on 12th May 1980.

There are claims that this station is haunted: In 1986,

Moulsecoomb Station looking west, 2007. Photo: Paul O'Callaghan

two young women decided to have a break from walking at 3.00am in the station waiting room. Whilst there, they were terrified by, firstly, an old man walking over the footbridge - who suddenly vanished, never walking past them - and then by a noise of something like a screeching pig. Both women fled!

London Road (Brighton) Station
Just before the 63-yard Ditchling Tunnel, the Kemp Town branch once ran (from 2nd August 1862 until June 1971, although it lost its passenger service back in 1932), which shall be explored in Volume Two. Peter A Harding has written a good booklet on the branch, which ran half on a viaduct and then through a tunnel. London Road (Brighton) Station opened on 1st October 1877. Most of the trains stopping here originally ran to and from Kemp Town. It has staggered platforms (not opposite each other), which are linked by a subway, the footbridge being part of a public right of way. The up platform is 459 ft long, whilst the down platform is 449 ft long. It has never had goods facilities. Though a white wall remains on the down platform, with modern shelters in front of it, the original station building here has gone, having been of a standard design similar to that at Hampden Park.

London Road (Brighton) Station, looking west, 2006. Photo: Paul O'Callaghan

The good news is that the more impressive up platform building survives (and has a twin at Worthing), though its main canopy has gone. The station building is at platform level, so a few steps lead up to it at the front, with the front canopy still remaining. A signal box existed at the west end of the down platform, overseeing four carriage sidings opposite, on the north side.

Immediately upon leaving London Road, passengers looking south can see the massive roof of Brighton Station, as the line curves to the left over the grand London/Preston Road viaduct, described earlier on page 11.

Unit 3053 RCYS Rail Tour crossing the London/Preston Road viaduct into Brighton, 8th April 1972. Photo: John Scrace

Brighton Station on 9th October 1932. Loco 794, 'Lady Dalziel', can be seen with the 11.05 'Southern Belle' from London Victoria. Photo: H C Casserley

Brighton Station

Built on the western slopes of the valley (causing engineering difficulties in its construction) in May 1840, this station had a small building to start with, mainly for clerks, enclosed by a wall. The goods station was on the east side. It was 130 ft above sea level and built by 3,500 men and 570 horses.

The station building (which survives today as the front of the present one) did not start construction until October 1840. It was designed by David Mocatta (not an L&BR employee). Like the SER stations at Ham street, Appledore and Rye, the

Brighton station building is also of Italianate design.

The platforms were covered by an overall roof, which was lower than the current example. The originals were by the L&BR's own engineer, John Rastrick. Each was 250 ft long (one roof for the Shoreham branch and two for the London line) and cast iron columns held up the wrought iron roof.

When the Lewes and Hastings line opened, three trains would depart at around 7.00am: one train going left, one straight ahead, and the remaining one to the right. In 1853 the platforms were lengthened, and thus the junction

Loco 803 leaves Brighton for London Victoria on 30th April 1932. On the left is the loco works office building. Photo: H C Casserley

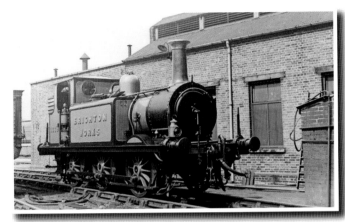

Brighton works yard, 28th June 1947, with its official locomotive, 3779, a 'Terrier' class engine. Photo: H C Casserley

between the Shoreham and main line tracks fell between the tracks, Platform 3 now being the only platform which could serve both lines. New platforms were added in 1860.

The present overall roof was by H E Wallis, but constructed under the overall control of Rastrick's successor, F D Bannister, in 1882-3. It was constructed above Rastrick's roof before this was dismantled, and consists of two spans supported by tall, slim, iron columns. It is internally decorated with spandrels and beams. The internal arched

The entrance to Brighton Station in 2006. Wallis' overall roof can be seen rising behind Mocatta's station building. Photo: Paul O'Callaghan

The porte-cochère (awning/massive canopy) at the front of the station and around its east side was added as part of the 1881-2 rebuild, even stretching over the forecourt (which extends over Trafalgar Street). During Dr Richard Beeching's reign in the early 1960s, there was a proposal to resite the station slightly to the north of the existing one, but this was not pursued. In 1971, Platform 10 was abolished after the Kemp Town branch was shut to freight, and a car park replaced the locomotive works. In December 1979, a new travel centre opened and, in 1980, a new ticket office.

Brighton thus makes a grand end to this important line.

Inside Brighton Station, 2002, with its classic roof. Photo: Paul O'Callaghan

roof supports the pitched roof, giving the outside impression that the roof has gables. It was at this time that the clock over the concourse was erected.

Because there was no more room for new platforms, it was from the 1880s that new signalling was installed so that two trains could use the same platform. In total the station had 11 platforms, Platform 9 being of mainly wooden build due to it being above the valley! When electrification of the main line took place in 1932, the former bay platform (No. 4) was abolished, as some of the other platforms were lengthened to take twelve-carriage trains.

Volume Two of *East Sussex Coastal Railways*

This concludes our exploration of the Ashford to Brighton railway and the fascinating histories of the many stations along its way. However, there are, of course, many other branches and narrow gauge railways that connect, or once connected, with this important line (for instance, Lewes Road to Kemp Town - siding from 1956 seen above, photo by H C Casserley). These will be explored in Volume Two of this series - *East Sussex Coastal Railways: Branch Lines and Other Railways*

About the Author

Paul O'Callaghan was born in New Eltham, London, and moved to Eastbourne in 2005. He first became interested in railways around 1986.

In 1994, when leaving sixth form, Paul O'Callaghan had three options: to go into journalism; join the Police (his preferred option); or do science and biology courses and train to be a doctor. Instead, he was struck down by a disabling infection, which damaged his balance organs.

The legal battle to obtain official treatment for the condition has robbed Paul's mother of their house, and he still suffers from constant rocking vertigo. He was finally diagnosed with paresis of the inner ear and vestibular neuronitis in 2002, but no treatment was offered and the extent of the damage remains uninvestigated. After many years of trying to find his own treatment, Paul is now too old to undertake medical training, and journalism will be hazardous, as too many hours are spent at computers. Paul has instead been campaigning for funds to set up his own health and research centre for the medically neglected, although he still hasn't given up hope of becoming a police officer.

Despite all this, Paul has managed to have articles published in local railway and history newsletters, books and railway magazines, as well as a local history journal, in which he has also had photos published. A dozen draft pages from this book were displayed at the Marshlink Rail Festival in September 2007.

Alexander Forbes

Paul O'Callaghan

Loco 283 at Rye, 11th April 1931. Photo: H C Casserley

S B Publications

For details of other fascinating books by S B Publications on East and West Sussex and other counties of south-east England, please visit our website:

www.sbpublications.co.uk

Or contact us at: 14 Bishopstone Road, Seaford, East Sussex, BN25 2UB
Tel: 01323 893498   Email: *sbpublications@tiscali.co.uk*